THE INDUS SCRIPT
A POSITIONAL STATISTICAL APPROACH

by

Michael Pieter Korvink

ISBN: 978-0-6151-8239-1
Rights Owner: Michael Korvink
Copyright: © 2008
Language: English
Country: United States
Edition: 2nd Edition

ACKNOWLEDGEMENTS

I am deeply indebted to Dr. J. Daniel White, my professor and friend, not only for sparking my interest in South Asian studies but for his guidance, encouragement, and tutelage. I sincerely thank Dr. John C. Reeves for his uncanny eye for detail and his profound linguistic knowledge. Finally, I thank my wife, Jen, for her endless love and encouragement as I wrote this work.

TABLE OF CONTENTS

PREFACE

There is a great difficulty for researchers as their understanding of the Indus inscriptions

changes. That is, they find themselves trying, in researching previous decipherment attempts, to

separate the observations from the inferences based upon those observations. Often observation and

inference are so tightly intertwined that they must start from scratch in their own research.[1] For

example, Mahadevan and Parpola have exhaustively researched positional-statistical patterns in the

script. However, much of their work intertwines linguistic terminology with positional-statistical

terminology (e.g. gender or nominative case suffixes). While the hard data of decipherment attempts,

such as the patterns in placement of various signs, remain constant, the conclusions drawn from that

data may become outdated.

I decided to prepare this thesis in response to this dilemma. Hence, the following thesis is

divided into four parts. The first of these (Chapter 1) is a general introduction to the nature of the

Indus script. This will include a basic setting up of parameters—how frequency and syntax are used,

the advantages and disadvantages of using a concordance, an explanation for abandoning the common

Dravidian approaches, and on a larger scale, the syllabic nature of the script itself.

The second section (Chapter 2) consists of a fresh examination of the hard data. From this

examination a tentative model for the script will be presented. This will rely heavily on the published

concordances and the archaeological record. One might use the second part of this essay as a research

tool for studying the various individual signs and their combinations. The patterns and rules of

---

[1] A discussion of previous decipherment attempts will be avoided here. For a thorough history of previous contributions to understanding the Indus Script, see Gregory L. Possehl, *Indus Age: The Writing System* (Philadelphia: University of Pennsylvania Press, 1996).

individual signs, pairwise combinations, trigrams, and other polygrams will be discussed in this section. Hence the would-be decipherer could use these pre-extricated units for *a priori* approaches, so common in this field.[2]

Many scholars in their discussion of Indus signs avoid labeling concrete patterns in the script. Instead, they may say that sign "A" is *commonly*, but not *always*, seen in the initial position. It will be shown in the following essay that the placement of signs is not as flexible as scholars previously believed. Rather than making generalizations, the use of a "thick description" of signs and groups of signs will be used. In this, the patterns of signs with a significant frequency will be discussed. Those inscriptions that are not in agreement with the pattern will be treated on an individual basis.

Next, (Chapter 3) the model thus derived will be applied to a number of inscriptions. Often would-be decipherers have presented plausible models. However, no decipherer has successfully *applied* his or her model. The reason for this failure may perhaps be due to their simultaneous pursuit for meaning and structure. This is surely a daunting task. But, since this model is only concerned with structure, the most speculative aspect of the script (its meaning) is put aside. Therefore, this model is grounded much more in concrete data.

Finally, the last section (Chapter 4) will discuss of some possible functions of the script in light of this re-examination. Statistical observation may allow us to narrow the search for the functions of the inscriptions. A discussion of the narrative, administrative, economic, and votive functions of the inscriptions will be found in this portion of the study.

---

[2] One may ask: If the Indus script does not represent language, why would these preextricated units be used for *a priori* approaches? One could use these units to look at *themes* that may have survived, much like John E. Mitchiner's suggestion of "The Seven High Places," rather than an underlying linguistic structure.

CHAPTER 1: THE NATURE OF THE INDUS SCRIPT

This thesis advocating a positional-statistical approach to the decipherment of the Indus script is of course dependent upon on a concordance. Thus it is necessary to discuss the drawbacks and benefits of such an approach. The concordance published by Iravatham Mahadevan has been the primary reference tool consulted in this thesis.[3] This is not to disparage the value of Asko Parpola's concordances,[4] which are of equal importance, but rather a single concordance has been used to maintain consistency in the study.

There are some drawbacks to the study of a concordance. One must fully accept the redactor's decisions regarding the "lumping" and "splitting" of signs into variants and functionally different signs. The lumping of two signs that are functionally different could have serious consequences in the concordance. For example, if a sign having an initial function were mistakenly cataloged as a variant of another sign having a medial function, the statistics for the sign, now erroneously combined in the concordance, would be corrupted. Consequently the statistics of that particular sign and all of its occurrences in the catalogued inscriptions are rendered useless.

A much simpler drawback can occur. One must trust that the concordance has accurately represented the inscription. The majority of the Indus inscriptions can be represented linearly in a concordance without much difficulty. Yet, other times, the linear order of a number of inscriptions

---

[3] Iravatham Mahadevan, *The Indus Script: Texts, Concordance and Tables* (New Delhi: K.P. Puthran at Tata Press Limited, 1977).

[4] Jagat Pati Joshi and Asko Parpola, eds., *Corpus of Indus Seals and Inscriptions: Collections in India* (Helsinki: Suomalainen Tiedeakatemia, 1987); Sayid Ghulam Mustafa Shah and Asko Parpola, eds., *Corpus of Indus Seals and Inscriptions: Collections in Pakistan* (Helsinki: Suomalainen Tiedeakatemia, 1991).

must be interpreted. For example, in the case of boustrophedon writing,[5] one may see two lines of script, each with their own linear order. This happens when a scribe, coming to the end of the object being engraved, wraps the text so that the first line is right-to-left while the second line is left-to-right.

Misrepresentation may occur another way. All lines of script, even those inscriptions where the script is written vertically, are presented horizontally in a concordance (though vertical inscriptions are indicated by the numerical code corresponding with each inscription).

Yet there are great benefits that offset these difficulties. With a computerized concordance, scholars have a standardized resource to use. One can, easily, check another scholar's work with access to the same concordance. Of course it would be much better if one could do positional-statistical studies by analyzing the inscriptions individually. Yet this is close to impossible, for surely the human error in compiling and analyzing the inscriptions, without forming a "font" or a concordance, would outnumber the benefits.

Moreover, variations of signs can often have only a minor difference in pictography while having a separate denotation. In the proposed positional-statistical approach, it is the *function* that is being investigated. Therefore, if two signs, which have the same syntactical function and different denotation are mistakenly combined as one by the compiler of the concordance, little harm is done for the purposes of this thesis. It would be similar to confusing the "?" and "!" signs in western scripts. While the syntax and function (being sentence ending markers) remains the same for these two characters, there is significant variation in the meaning (i.e, question and exclamation). Problems would only occur, in respect to this study, when signs having different syntactical functions are combined. The combination of variants which frequently occurs is the assimilation of a sign that has slight pictographic variation and a low frequency with a sign that is thought to be the most common rendering of the sign, having a relatively high frequency. This is not to say that this mistake has not happened—after all it is an undeciphered script—but rather it is to suggest that the signs examined here

---

[5] The term "boustrophedon" refers to writing that changes direction due the curling of the script to the next line.

have shown little variation in function, implying a carefully chosen set of basic signs by the compiler. Any evidence suggesting an accidental "lumping" of functionally different signs will be discussed.

I would note that there has been no effort in this thesis to separate functionally different objects (for example, separating seals from copper implements). In an analysis of objects with a shared pattern of signs, one is also analyzing a shared function of the objects. One could use the example of envelopes and street addresses. On an envelope in the United States, for example, one can see a consistent pattern in the sequencing of a street address: destination name, numerical prefix, name of the street, suffix for the street (e.g. Dr., Ave. etc.), city, state, numerical suffix (zip code) and an optional ending for the country (if it is to go outside the United States). Envelopes exhibiting an inscription with the above structure could easily be distinguished from the writing on the letter inside. Analyzing documents (envelopes) which share this structure would also be an examination of functionally similar objects. Hence one can infer that the identification of inscribed objects sharing similar patterns would also be an identification of objects with a similar function. However, as a general rule of thumb, the great majority of the objects sharing the same pattern in this thesis are seals and sealings.

1.1 The Tools of Frequency and Syntax

There are a number of methods that may be employed in order to extricate separate units of information from an inscription. They include 1) frequency of pairwise combinations, 2) strong and weak bonds, and 3) the process of elimination. These will be discussed below.

An examination of Mahadevan's concordance shows that there are many pairwise combinations which occur with a high frequency. The majority of these have little significant value due to their pairing with terminal endings and initial signs. For example, the "jar," acting as a terminal marker and being the most frequent sign, will have a high frequency of occurrences with many other signs, though it likely does not denote a separate idea. Similarly, high frequencies of pairs containing a prefixing sign often may be dismissed as having little syntactical value. Frequency may be helpful, for example, on a seal where three unknown signs are read in a row. Hypothetically speaking, if A and B are seen sixty times in a separate context while B and C are seen together only on two separate occasions, it is worth further investigating A and B as a pair, assuming no suffixes (e.g. ꝟ , ꝉ , 𝌆 , etc.) or prefixes

(e.g. " ◇). One might then ask other questions about the pair in question. For example, does the

pair occur in isolation on an inscription? If so, it might be inferred that they stand as a separate unit of

information.

It is also necessary to compare the frequency of the individual signs to the frequency of the

pair. If A and B are thought to be a pair due to their relatively high pairwise frequency, it is necessary

to compare the individual frequencies of A and B to the frequency of the pair. If both signs have

individual frequencies over 100 and the pair frequency is 6, it is not a high enough proportion to be

helpful. That is not to say that it is not a pairwise combination. Rather, the frequency is simply not

high enough to be able to determine if it is or if it is not. On the other hand, if B has a frequency of 10,

C has a frequency of 100 and the pairs are seen together 9 times, it is known that nine out of ten times

B occurs with the BC pair.

This is demonstrated below. The numbers above the letters (representing Indus script signs)

illustrate the individual frequency of the sign, while the numbers below the letters illustrate the

pairwise frequency of the two signs:[6]

WEAK PAIRWISE COMBINATION

102   163

A   B

6

MEDIUM PAIRWISE COMBINATION

10   100

B   C

9

---

[6] It is necessary to add that there is not a standard frequency that determines a strong or weak bond. The strength is a matter of degree.

STRONG PAIRWISE COMBINATION

17   15

D   E

15

This same method for isolating pairwise combinations has also been suggested by Asko Parpola

as seen in the following quote:

> The strength of the joint between two successive signs can be estimated if we count the
> number of occurrences of both the individual signs and the pairs of these signs in the
> whole corpus. We call joints strong where the pairwise frequency is significantly higher
> than what would be expected on the basis of the total frequencies of the individual
> signs. It can be argued that inside grammatical forms, the joints tend to be strong, and
> between forms, weak. Now if we count the frequencies from the raw corpus, any pair
> of signs occurring in a heavily repeated text will signal a strong joint.[7]

Once one successfully isolates a pair or set of three or four signs, it is useful to find their

repetition in other contexts; for example, their occurrences with other prefixing (initial) and terminal

signs. This proves much more helpful than an entire inscription being repeated where there is no

difference in context for the signs in question (duplicates).

The process of elimination may also be used to extricate individual units of information from

an inscription. Steven Christopher Bonta suggests this method for segmentation. To quote his

argument:

> Using the comparative method to isolate verbal units, we may state the following rules,
> using sign sequences DCBA, DC, BA, DCFE, and FE:
> 1) If we have DCBA and DC, then we read as DC BA; furthermore, we may expect to
>   find BA.
> 2) If we have DCBA and DCFE, then we read DC BA and DC FE; furthermore, we may
>   expect to find DC, BA, and FE.
> Restated a sign sequence in isolation compared with the same sequence within a longer
> inscription suggests isolation of that sequence as a verbal unit within the longer sequence.[8]

Though Bonta is probably mistaken in using this technique for identifying an underlying language in

the Indus inscriptions, his method for extricating units of information is noteworthy.

---

[7] Kimmo Koskenniemi and Asko Parpola, *Documentation and Duplicates of the texts in the Indus Script*, Research Reports No. 2, (Helsinki: University of Helsinki, 1980), 52-53.

[8] Steven Christopher Bonta, *Topics in the Study of the Indus Valley Script* (M.A. thesis, Brigham Young University, 1996), 17.

Basically, Bonta is suggesting that a process of elimination can be used to isolate meaningful sequences of signs in the Indus inscriptions. One might add to Bonta's rules that the isolation of BA from DC in DCBA may also be broken down into B and A as separate ideas. That is to say, one should not rule out the possibilities of single signs representing separate ideas in the inscription. An examination of the strength or weakness of the bond would supply insight as to whether BA is a pairwise combination or whether they are in fact separate units of information, being B and A.

I will argue that a majority of the most frequent signs in the script have a consistent placement in lines of texts. Signs $\mathcal{V}$, $\mathcal{\hat{T}}$ and $\mathbb{B}$ and their variants are a few of the best-known examples of terminals; i.e., they occur most frequently at the end of a line of text. The sign termed "fish" (and all its variations) has a greater medial frequency, while $\diamondsuit$ and $\otimes$ exhibit a high frequency in the initial placement.[9]

For the majority of the signs, however, it is difficult to establish patterns due to their extremely low frequency. Statistics from Mahadevan's concordance reinforce this observation:[10]

Frequency of Range	Number of signs
1000 or more	1
999-500	1
499-100	31
99-50	34
49-10	86
9-2	152
Only once	112

Figure 1: Range Frequency of Signs

The signs in the frequency range of (1) and (2-9) are of weak statistical value. Yet if one exempts these ranges from the analysis, one must ignore roughly 63% of the characters. Therefore the majority of this analysis would rely on the remaining 37% of the inscriptions! On a positive note, many of these lower frequency signs are graphic variants of more frequent signs. Because this essay is

---

[9] The use of the term "fish" for these characters is not to imply that they actually represent fish. This term is simply a reference tool. Also, from this point on the quotations will be dropped.

[10] Mahadevan, Concordance, 17.

not an investigation of meaning, but rather of function, one may assume that more frequent signs give insight to their less frequent variants.

1.2 The Nonsyllabic Nature of the Indus Script

It will be argued in the following that there are syntactical rules for the order of signs in the Indus script. One might at first suggest that since language has grammatical rules, it would make sense that the Indus script, having order, could represent a language. Yet, this may not be true. The order of the signs of the script ironically argues against the script as a type of logo-syllabic script. It is known that logo-syllabic (word-syllable) scripts operate by piecing together syllables to yield phonetic representation of the words. To use a hypothetical example, let us take the phonetic pieces "res" and "car." One could combine them to form a phonetic representation of the phrase "race-car." These pieces may, in turn, be reversed to yield the word "caress." Hence, in a logo-syllabic script, one would expect to see various phonic pieces prefixing and suffixing other signs. If one studies the terminal, medial, and prefixing signs, it is clear that there is a fixed order to those signs in the script. Hence the alleged phonic pieces can only be used in a set position in relation to others.

One might raise the point that a strict linear placement of some signs in relation to others signs may very well be seen in languages. For example, a language may allow "dr̥" and "ta" to form "dr̥ta," but may not allow the reversal "tadr̥."[11] This aspect of the language could then be reflected in the placement of signs in the script. However, with the medial "fish" signs, for example, *five* signs may be seen in a set relative order. Having five signs rather than two (e.g. dr̥ta) in a hierarchical order complicates the suggestion that this may be reflected in language. Let us say that the letters below represent a fixed order of syllabic signs in hypothetical script X:

A B C D E

If we assume that the signs in script X are sound syllables and have a fixed positional order, language X would be quite strange. One could, with "A," make the combinations AB, AC, AD, and AE. However, with "D," one could only make the combination DE and *never* DC, DB, or DA.

---

[11] I would like to thank Hans Hock for bringing this point to my attention.

Furthermore, *no* phonetic combinations of E with A, B, C, or D would be allowed. Such an ordering of sound syllables is difficult to imagine in a language. It has been suggested, based *solely* on the number of signs, that the Indus script is logo-syllabic. Hence a conflict arises for a logo-syllabic script that also has a fixed order. Trying to determine the nature of a script based on the total number of signs is a helpful tool. Yet it is, at the same time, speculative. Examining the positional pattern of the signs, as stated above, allows one to minimize speculation. Thus if the Indus script has a fixed order (as seen in the "fish" and terminals), the script *cannot* be logo-syllabic. Further corroboration to this argument is supplied by the recent work of Steve Farmer.

In a recent presentation at the fifth annual Harvard Indology roundtable meeting, Steve Farmer presented an abridged form of a larger forthcoming paper which addresses the question of whether the Indus inscriptions reflected "encoded speech."[12] Through a series of arguments, Farmer concludes that the Indus inscriptions were not representative of speech. His arguments will be briefly discussed here.

The first case examines a number of common cultural "markers" used by societies with manuscript traditions. Those societies that do not have these "markers" do not have manuscript traditions. His study is a response to the idea that the Indus civilization may have had longer texts on perishable material. He suggests that if the Indus civilization did have longer documents, one should be able to find a number of "markers" in the archaeological record that would be suggestive of this manuscript tradition. These correlations are based on a number of civilizations including those of South Asia, Mesopotamia, Anatolia, the Aegean, Egypt, China, and Mesoamerica. In these traditions, "markers" suggestive of a manuscript tradition have been found. However, none is to be found in the Indus civilization.

His next argument examines the frequencies of the fifty most common Indus script signs. He asserts that, when compared with a number of logo-syllabic scripts, the Indus script, in respect to sign occurrences, seems to be largely syllabic in content. However, with a closer analysis, one may see that

---

[12] Steve Farmer, "Five Cases of 'Dubious Writing' in Indus Inscriptions: Parallels with Vinča Symbols and Cretan Hieroglyphic Seals," Handout from the Fifth Harvard University Roundtable, available from http://www.safarmer.com/downloads, accessed February 25, 2004.

sign repetition in other logo-syllabic scripts and that of the Indus script is quite different—the Indus script shows very little repetition when compared to logo-syllabic scripts. This corroborates the argument against the Indus script as encoded speech.

He continues to build on this thesis with the cooperation of Richard Sproat.[13] They argue that the discovery of new unseen Indus signs is directly proportional to the discovery of new inscriptions. In a typical logo-syllabic language one can expect to find, with the discovery of more inscriptions, more occurrences of those signs with a previously low frequency. Hence at some point the discovery of unseen signs should reach a plateau, regardless of the amount of new findings. This is not the case for the Indus inscriptions. Over the last few decades, new signs continue to appear with the discovery of new inscriptions. This again argues against understanding the Indus script as encoded speech. These three points—all quite different in their approach, yet in agreement—give almost irrefutable evidence for the non-syllabic nature of the Indus script.

1.3 Previous Methods

There are many previous contributions to the study of the Indus script that deserve a re-examination. Often the theory underlying an analysis of the inscriptions is interwoven with the analysis itself. Thus difficulties arise in extricating the objective information from material motivated by the theory. The following is an examination of some of the contributions from previous scholars to the idea of the positional-statistical approach. The observations which I highlight have been carefully selected, being only those that I consider are worth a fresh examination. This section is hence not an exhaustive review of their works.

After such an examination of these various observations, it will be seen that there is much agreement among these decipherment attempts with respect to the structure of the script. Each of these attempts—using quite different terminology and having a quite different understanding of the Indus people—dance around the same patterns in the script.

---

[13] Richard W. Sproat, *A Computational Theory of Writing Systems* (Cambridge: Cambridge University Press, 2000).

Let us begin with the Soviet decipherment attempt.[14] The Soviet decipherment attempt is a rather technical compilation of essays, difficult to digest by the mildly interested scholar or student of the Indus script. The criticisms of their methods are many. To name a few, the control script or language which they reference (they make little distinction between the two) is Egyptian. Based solely on the number of characters, one would expect the choice of a logo-syllabic script as a control, yet they chose Egyptian hieroglyphs, a pictographic script. Furthermore, Egyptian texts, which are largely narrative in function, are here compared with a script in which the inscriptions rarely total more than ten signs. They simply string the Indus inscriptions together to make a longer inscription. Of course the more critical problem with the Soviet method is their search for the *language* of the script. Arlene Zide and Kamil Zvelebil have critiqued these essays quite extensively. Redundancy of their arguments will be avoided here. Rather, I will look at their studies of the script more optimistically.

A. M. Kondratov in his article "The Positional-Statistical Analysis of the Proto-Indian Texts"[15] discusses three elements in the Indus script—what he terms *root signs, variable signs,* and semi-*variable signs.*[16] According to Kondratov, a *root sign* maintains a rather consistent placement with a line of text. For example, one can say that the "jar" ᴜF or "arrow" ᐱ maintains a consistent final placement in a line of script. Next are the *variable* and *semi-variable sign*s,

> The difference between the variable and semi-variable signs consists of the order of their mutual sequence. The variable sign always 'gives way' to the semi-variable sign in a block-polygram and follows after (in the case of suffixation) or [precedes] before (in the case of prefixation) the semi-variable. Thus the semi-variable signs behave as if they 'pushed aside' the variable signs from the root-signs and polygrams.[17]

---

[14] Arlene R. K. Zide and Kamil V. Zvelebil, eds., *The Soviet Decipherment of the Indus Valley Script: Translation and Critique* (The Hague: Mouton, 1976).

[15] A. M. Kondratov, "The Positional-Statistical Analysis of the Proto-Indian Texts," in *The Soviet Decipherment of the Indus Valley Script: Translation and Critique,* eds. Arlene R. K Zide and Kamil V. Zvelebil (The Hague: Mouton, 1976), 39-48.

[16] Many of the articles in the Soviet volume are cryptically written. In the case of Kondratov's article, Indus signs are referred to by the number given to them in the excavation reports of Marshall and Mackay (John Marshall, *Mohenjo-Daro and the Indus Civilization*. 3 Vols. [London: Arthur Probsthain, 1931]; Ernest Mackay, *Further Excavations at Mohenjo-daro*. 2 Vols. [Delhi: Government of India, 1937-1938]). If one looks these up, however, it will be seen that some of the numbers given by Kondratov do not have signs corresponding to them in the excavation reports. For example, Kondratov list signs 500 and 501 as variable signs while 507 is given as a semi-variable. Yet, when one attempts to look these up, he or she will find that Langdon's sign list ends at 288 (vol. 1 in Marshall), Marshall's sign-manual ends at 396 (vol. 3) and Mackay's sign manual ends at 450 (vol.2). Therefore the combinations that list these signs have been omitted from this study.

[17] Ibid., 44.

Y. V. Knorozov, in "The Formal Analysis of the Proto-Indian Script,"[18] uses similar terminology, though he gives a bit more clarity. He defines these terms as follows:

> The signs may be classified as stable, variable, and semi-variable. Stable signs are preserved in all cases, when the given block occurs, and obviously, they express root-morphemes. In the structure of a block one to two stable signs occur. Semi-variable ('block-forming') signs may be divided into two sharply differing groups: the semi-variables of the first group occur before the stable ones; and the semi-variables of the second group occur after the stable ones but before the variables. Thus, they are retained within the limits of the entire micro-paradigm. The variable ('block-altering') signs always occur after the stable signs and after the second group. They can be interchanged with each other; they can be combined in pairs; they can disappear, forming a micro-paradigm; obviously, they perform the function of suffixes in the Proto-Indian language.[19]

The example given by Kondratov will be paraphrased here. Take the hypothetical inscriptions abx, aby, abkx, abxy, abrx, and abry. "a" and "b" would be the root signs, "x" and "y" would be the variable signs and "k" and "r" would be semi-variables. Hence there are two levels of contingency.

There are many problems in the article that will not be discussed here. Let us simply pull out this useful bit of information from the article and analyze it. What Kondratov is suggesting is that there is an linear order of priority in the signs. In other words, some signs take priority in the adjacent position. The placement of semi-variable signs is contingent on the existence of a variable sign. Hence if we return to the above example, one would not find the inscription "abr," for the occurrence of "r" is contingent on that of an "x" or "y." While the model is quite useful for the present study, the examples as used in Kondratov's article are not worth repeating. The pairwise combinations and polygrams that Kondratov lists are statistically weak. Rather than using the examples given by Kondratov, the text below will employ this framework with the benefit of current data to show how "constant" (root or stable signs, if you wish) and "variable signs" can be identified in the Indus script. It will be shown that such components do exist in initial, medial and terminal signs. To see this applied, see the sections below on the "fish" signs and "terminal signs".

Walter Fairservis also utilizes the idea of a syntactical priority of signs in the script. In his The Harappan Civilization and its Writing, he presents a grid where a number of individual inscriptions are

---

[18] Yu. V. Knorozov, "The Characteristics of the Language of the Proto-Indian Inscriptions," in *The Soviet Decipherment of the Indus Valley Script*, 55-59.

[19] Ibid., 56.

shown and where he attempts to show the similarity in positional placement among the various inscriptions. There are a number of difficulties with this grid. While one may see the positional consistency of signs in the initial position on the right and signs with a terminal frequency on the left in his grid, only nineteen of the almost three thousand extant[20] inscriptions are accounted for. Any selection of this size will surely be a biased representation of the patterns in the script.

In the present study, various grids will be presented that take into account all of the inscriptions, thus avoiding a biased representation of the inscriptions. Prefixes, medial information, and terminals will be given a "thick description." This essay will put signs under the microscope. Fish signs, rather than being lumped into one positional slot, will be further broken down. Similarly, terminal signs will be assigned a positional slot in relation to each other rather than being lumped under one column.

It is also helpful to look at the structural model proposed by Iravatham Mahadevan. While his model assumes an underlying language to the script, the structural elements of the model are significant. An inscription in his model may contain up to five possible components.[21] Let us look at the examples given by Mahadevan:

	E	D	C	B	A
1078	Ꝣ	朳	人	"	◇
1543	⻗	乤	屮	⁾	⊗

AB- Attributive (introductory phrase)
A- Substantive (of the attributive phrase)
B- Case-maker suffix (attached to substantive)
CDE- Substantive (main phrase of the text)
C- Attributes to the substantive D
D- Substantive root morpheme of the main phrase
E- Normal suffix (attached to substantive D)

---

[20] Walter A. Fairservis, *The Harappan Civilization and its Writing: A Model for the Decipherment of the Indus Script* (New Delhi: Oxford University Press & IBH Publishing, 1992), 226.
[21] Iravatham Mahadevan, "Toward a Grammar of the Indus Texts: 'Intelligible to the Eye, it not to the Ears," in *Tamil Civilization* 4. 3-4 (1986): 27.

Thus an inscription may be divided into two sections. Disregarding the fact that this is a linguistic term, the first of these is the "attributive" section. The placement of sign A is contingent on the presence of sign B. Together they form a prefixing unit denoting a separate idea.

Secondly is the "substantive" section. Here E and C qualify the "root morpheme" D. There are some difficulties in this part of the model. Rather than having E and C qualify D, the suffix (or terminal) should be thought of as a separate unit. There is no evidence that suggests that E should have any syntactical relationship to D or C.

Most recently, Steven Christopher Bonta has presented a structural model for the Indus inscriptions.[22] He concludes (like Mahadevan and Parpola), with similar techniques of frequency and syntax, that the Indus inscriptions have a terminal class, a medial class, and a prefixing class (though their arguments vary in diction). An inscription segmented by Bonta, is listed below.

#1620, 2:

Terminal sign   Root cluster   Fish sign   Terminal   Prefix

Bonta is clearly on the right track in the construction of his model. Though he also assumes an underlying language in the Indus inscriptions, his analysis is easily removable from his interpretation of the analysis. That is to say, the above segmentation does not have blatant linguistic implications.

Bonta's model basically assumes a terminal class, various medial classes, and a prefixing class. With this classification as a starting point, let us now turn to the model which I will propose in this thesis.

---

[22] Bonta, *Topics in the Study of the Indus Valley Script.*
[23] Ibid., 105.

CHAPTER 2: THE STRUCTURAL MODEL

From the previous chapter, one can see that many have proposed models for a linear order in the Indus script. While scholars have made some progress in the positional-statistical field of the Indus script, none of the models has proven successful when applied.

Let us now turn to the new model proposed in this thesis (see Appendix A). The dotted line, on the chart, is representative of a line of text. The arrow illustrates the right-to-left order of the script.[24] The characters comprising a line will be presented and discussed in the following order.

The first element of a line of text is the "prefixing element." This would be a close equivalent of Mahadevan's "attributive" or "introductory phrase."[25] As discussed above, the "attributive" is comprised of a "substantive" and a "case-maker suffix." The Soviet terminology, though strictly speaking not analogous, may also be applied. As suggested by Kondratov, the placement of the "variable" sign must be contingent on the placement of the "constant" sign. As will be discussed, the placement of the variable sign is contingent on the constant sign. Together they constitute a "prefixing" compound. This will be explained below in the section on "prefixes."

Next, will be an examination of the "terminal" signs—perhaps the most widely discussed aspect of the script. Though one major class of terminals will be presented, two minor classes will also be discussed. All three classes exhibit a linear order. Since prefixing and terminal elements will be used to isolate medial signs, they will be discussed first.

---

[24] Due to the presence of boustrophedon writing, cramping and overlapping of the Indus characters, is assumed that the script is read from right to left. For a thorough discussion on this, see *Indus Age: The Writing System*, 59.

[25] Iravatham Mahadevan, "Toward a Grammer of the Indus Texts," 27.

The next elements to be discussed are the medial signs and compounds—B1, B2 and B3. These three elements exhibit no fixed order in relation to each other. For example, "numeral" signs may be seen before or after the "fish" signs.

Each of the elements comprising medial signs will be discussed individually. First will be an analysis of the so-called "fish" signs. While there seems to be no relative linear order to the "numerals," "fish" and other medial signs, linear order occurs within the "fish." It will be demonstrated that certain "fish" must be placed before or after other fish signs. In other words, there is a linear hierarchy to the fish signs. Hence this section will examine the positional-statistical patterns of the fish signs.

The signs and sign compounds listed under the "other medial signs" exhibit no fixed syntactical relationship to other signs, other than that they have a medial placement and have been extricated as individual units by the aforementioned tools of frequency and syntax. Therefore, discussion of these signs and compounds focuses mainly on the strength of the joint between the two signs.

Finally those signs, commonly considered to be numeral signs will be discussed. There are many signs and sign combinations that can be thought of as possible signs for numerals. As stated earlier, the objective of this study is to extricate and analyze the patterns in frequency and syntax of the signs. A search for meaning lies outside the scope of this study, but the assignment of a quantitative value to the signs falls into the category of meaning. Hence the separation of the numeral signs can be somewhat arbitrary with respect to the positional-statistical approach. This separation has been effected mainly for neatness.

One must note that the inscriptions contain only the "necessary" information; any information which would have been obvious to the reader is lacking. For example, one inscription may contain a prefixing element, some medial information, and no terminal, while another inscription may have a terminal, medial information, and no prefix. Hence the inscriptions often vary in length.

2.1 Prefixing Signs

Many scholars have noted the regularity with which certain signs occur together. Most of their comments simply state that signs "x" and "y" occur together more frequently than other pairs of signs; the combination must signal be a separate idea. The following analysis will take this observation a step further by assigning a causative value to a sign, in the sense that one sign "causes" another adjacent sign to function differently. For example, "q" and "u" often occur together in English. While "u" can be seen functioning with or without "q," "q" is much less likely to be seen alone. One might synopsize this observation by stating that "q" is somewhat reliant on "u." But rather than simply stating that "q" and "u" occur together frequently, it should be said that "q" causes "u" to follow due to syllabic facilitation. It will be shown in the following study that ' , " and ') exhibit a similar causative value.[26]

Let us examine the syntax and frequency of five signs in the Indus script: ⚡, ᛝ , 𝟡 , ⊕ , ') . These can be seen in their context in the following four inscriptions:

⟨inscription⟩ [27]

⟨inscription⟩ [28]

⟨inscription⟩ [29]

⟨inscription⟩ [30]

Walter Fairservis has also observed the regularity of these pairwise combinations and concludes that they are likely to "share a common theme."[31] These pairwise combinations do in fact have a similar function. However, in addition to this observation, it will be argued that when ') occurs with ⚡, ᛝ , 𝟡 or ⊕ , the two signs, as a pairwise combination, change function to act as a prefix. When these four signs are seen independently of ') , they function much differently, as indicated by their medial placement.

---

[26] I do not mean to imply that the grammatical rule proposed here functions as syllabic facilitation, in the Indus script.

[27] All Indus script inscriptions are cited according to the system of annotation employed in Mahadevan's corpus; Ibid., 4056.

[28] Ibid., 1170.

[29] Ibid., 4404.

[30] Ibid., 1345.

[31] Walter A. Fairservis, *The Harappan Civilization and its Writing* (New Delhi: Oxford University Press), 80.

This being stated, let us now look at the positional frequency of ⟩ :

Solo	0
Initial	0
Medial	186
Final	7
Total	193

Here it can be seen that sign ⟩ never occurs alone or at the beginning of an inscription, although it does often directly follow a number of signs in the initial position as seen in the pairwise frequencies below:

Pairwise Combinations with		Pairwise Frequency
⟩	+ ⋈	44
⟩	+ K	23
⟩	+ ⟩	54
⟩	+ ⊗	24
		Total of 145 Occurrences

Figure 2: Common Prefixes Containing ⟩

Hence in one hundred forty-five out of its one hundred ninety-three occurrences, ⟩ is seen with four variable initial signs.[32] Signs in pairwise combination in the remaining forty-eight occurrences with ⟩ have been excluded due to their low frequency.

We must now look at how the signs function when not paired with ⟩ . Though any of the signs may be seen in the initial position without ⟩ , they are very rarely seen with ⟩ in a medial position, unless there is more than one unit of information listed in the line of text.[33] The analysis upon which this is based is shown below:

---

[32] I will use the term "variable initial sign" to refer to signs whose placement is contingent on the presence of a "constant" sign (e.g. K , ⟩ , ⊗).

[33] Multiple units of information within a line of script will be discussed later in the essay.

Sign ′) and ⋈

First one must look at the frequency of sign ⋈ :

Solo	2
Initial	36
Medial	49
Final	3
Total	90

Sign ′) is seen with ⋈ twenty-three out of the ninety times ′) occurs. Out of these twenty-three times they are seen together, sign ⋈ occurs in the initial placement twenty-one times. Of the two times they do not occur together, one of them is characterized as a doubtful reading by Mahadevan.[34] Moreover, the pairwise combination ′) and ⋈ , does not occur medially. Thus it can be said that the two signs in question have a consistent placement when occuring together as a pair, while an independent ⋈ may be placed in initial, medial, or in the final position. Hence, ⋈ in combination with ′) acts as a prefix (a constant and a variable).

Sign ′) and ⋇

The following is the positional breakdown of sign ⋇ .

Solo	0
Initial	51
Medial	11
Final	1
Total	63

As can be seen from the above chart, ′) appears with ⋇ forty-four times out of its sixty-three occurrences. In thirty-nine of these forty-four occurrences the pair occurs in the initial position. The remaining five pairs, though located in the medial position, continue to act as prefixes. Let us examine these inscriptions:

---

[34] Ibid., 1027.

ᚢ ᚠ ᛁ ᛞ ᛏ ᚫ ᚱ ᛫ ᚷ 35

ᚢ ᚢ ᛁ ᛞ ᚢ ᛞ ᛁ ᛞ ᛁ ᛞ 36

ᚫ ᛁ ᛞ ᛖ ᛖ ᚷ 37

ᚢ ᚠ ᛁ ᛞ ᛏ ᚫ ᚱ ᛫ ᚷ 38

ᚢ ᚢ ᛁ ᛞ ᚢ ᛞ ᛁ ᛞ ᛁ ᛞ 39

The medial placement of ᛁᛞ in inscriptions 1321, 2690, 2398, and 1012 may be easily explained. Using the prefixing and terminal elements in these inscriptions, one can separate them into two units of information. Therefore the medial occurrences of these prefixes are due simply to the multiple units of information contained in the inscription. Inscription 2016 is much more ambiguous. There exists the possibility that this functions as a polygramic prefix. In other words, ᛁ causes ᛖ , ᛖ and ᚷ (in addition to ᛞ), to assume the initial position. This possibility is discussed in greater detail below.

Hence it can be said that these five inscriptions (with the possible exception of 2016) are not in disagreement with our hypothesis but rather support the idea that sign ᛁ causes its pairwise sign to assume the initial position in a line of text. Again, when not occurring in a pairwise combination with ᛁ, ᛞ appears in the final and medial as well as the initial positions.

Sign ᛁ and ᚷ / Sign ᛁ and ⊕

These two signs are discussed together due to their similar positional statistics. On every occasion that sign ᛁ is paired with ᚷ or ⊕ , they appear in the initial position, while signs ᚷ and ⊕ may occur in the medial position when not paired with ᛁ . This again is indicative of these signs' dependency on ᛁ for an initial placement.

---

[35] Ibid., 1321.

[36] Ibid., 2690.

[37] Ibid., 2016.

[38] Ibid., 2398.

[39] Ibid., 1012.

From the above remarks it can be stated that sign ⟩ has a direct impact on the placement of ⋊, ⋇, ⟩ and ⊕ when occurring in pairwise combination. This knowledge of prefixes in conjunction with a knowledge of terminals can be used as a tool to separate previously indivisible inscriptions into more than one unit of information. To illustrate this, the prefix ⟩⋇[40] (consisting of a constant and a variable sign) and the terminal ⋎, often called the "jar" sign, can be used to distinguish two separate units of information in the following seal:

⋎ ⊛ ⟩⋇ ⋎ ⋇⋇ ⟩ ⋇ [41]

An essential approach to unraveling this inscription is to analyze each idea separately and not as one single strand of information. The ⋇'s coupled with sign ⟩ act as a prefix. Thus these medial positions are not functioning in a syntactically different way, but they continue to act as a prefix.

In summary, it can be seen that ⟩ clearly causes ⋊, ⋇, ⟩ and ⊕ to be placed initially within inscriptions. When these same four signs do not appear with , they may enjoy final and medial placement in addition to an initial placement.

In addition to ⟩, two other signs (' and '') cause ⋊, ⋇, ⟩, and ⊕ to assume an initial placement. For the purposes of this essay, they will be labeled the "single quotation" and "double quotation." The high frequency of initial placement of signs ⋊, ⋇, ⟩, and ⊕ when paired with ', '' and ⟩ can be seen in the following charts:

---

[40] Please note that ⋇ functions quite differently from ⋇ and should not be confused.
[41] Ibid., 2690.

SIGN ⊛			
Pairwise combination	Pairwise Frequency of combination	Pairwise Frequency in the Initial Position	Inscriptions to be explained
' ⊛	4	2	2
ı ⊛	14	12	2
" ⊛	83	76	9
'⟩ ⊛	24	24	0
Totals	125	113	13
List of the 13 inscriptions to be explained			
Inscriptions #	Inscription		
2069	𐤗 𐤖 𐤋 𐤅 ' ⊛ ⊚ ⊛ ⊛ ⊛		
1337	' ⊛ ⊟ 𐤅 𐤅 ⊞		
3067	𐤏 𐤋 ' ⊛ 𐤋 𐤗 ⊟		
2029	𐤅 ⟩ 𐤙 𐤋 ' ⊛ ⊛		
2463	𐤅 ⊕ " ⊛ 𐤅		
8029	𐤅 𐤛 𐤛 " ⊛ |||		
2130	𐤏 𐤒 || " ⊛ 𐤅		
2559	" ⊛)(		(damaged)
2208	𐤏 ||| 𐤅 𐤋 " ⊛ ∪		
3155	" ⊛ 𐤅 ⫶⫶		
2286	𐤙 𐤒	" ⊛ 𐤅		
2447	𐤅 𐤟 𐤅 𐤏 || " ⊛ 𐤅		
5325	" ⊛		(damaged)

Figure 3: Frequency Distribution of Prefixes Containing

SIGN ⋉			
Pairwise combination	Pairwise Frequency of combination	Pairwise Frequency in the Initial Position	Inscriptions to be explained
' ⋉	1	1	0
ı ⋉	2	2	0
" ⋉	N/A	N/A	N/A
'⟩ ⋉	23	21	2
Totals	26	24	2 (see below)
List of the 2 inscriptions to be explained			
Inscriptions #	Inscription		
1027	𐤅 𐤋 𐤅 √ 𐤗 '⟩ ⋉		
2406	𐤅 ⊛ || 𐤒 '⟩ ⋉ 𐤅 ⊚		

Figure 4: Frequency Distribution of Prefixes Containing ⋉

SIGN ✕			
Pairwise combination	Pairwise Frequency of combination	Pairwise Frequency in the Initial Position	Inscriptions to be explained
' ✕	1	1	0
ı ✕	1	1	0
" ✕	N/A	N/A	N/A
ʾ ✕	46	40	6
Totals	48	42	6
List of the 6 inscriptions to be explained			
Inscriptions #	Inscription		
2016	𐤗ʾ✕𐤄𐤄𐤣		
1321	ᚢ𐤀ʾ✕𐤕𐤀𐤀ıϑ		
2398	ᚢ𐤀ʾ✕𐤕𐤀𐤀ıϑ		
3221	ʾ✕ᚢ	(damaged)
2690	ᚢ☺ʾ✕ ᚢ𐤊√𐤗ʾ✕		
1012	ᚢ ☺ʾ✕ ᚢ𐤊√𐤗ʾ✕		

Figure 5: Frequency Distribution of Prefixes Containing ✕

SIGN ϑ			
Pairwise combination	Pairwise Frequency of combination	Pairwise Frequency in the Initial Position	Inscriptions to be explained
' ϑ	2	2	0
ı ϑ	1	0	1
" ϑ	7	0	7
ʾ ϑ	55	55	0
Totals	65	57	8
List of the 8 inscriptions to be explained			
Inscriptions #	Inscription		
2617	ᚔıᚔ ı ᚔᚔᚔᚒ𐤀'ϑ𐤊		
4349	𐤇ᚢ𐤊ᚢᚪ" ϑ◌		
7236	" ϑ𐤇	(damaged)
7219	" ϑ𐤇	(damaged)
3110	ᚢ𐤅ᚔᚔᚒ☺" ϑ𐤇		
7258	ᚢ𐤅𐤦𐤀" ϑ𐤇		
7251	" ϑ𐤇	(damaged)
6230	ᚢ ᚔᚔᚔ" ϑ𐤇		

Figure 6: Frequency Distribution of Prefixes Containing ϑ

Mahadevan makes a distinction between the "single quotation" seen close to the initial sign and the one that is somewhat removed.[42] Hence he lists ⟩⊗ and ⟩⊗ as separate pairwise combinations in his concordance. While the positional breakdown of this sign shows them in separate rows, they are understood to be *functionally* the same (in this essay), given their similar statistics.

The above breakdown has been formatted in this way for two reasons. Firstly, one may see that the great majority of pairwise combinations containing ' , " , and ⟩ assume the initial placement. Secondly, every inscription where the pairwise combination does not assume the initial placement is listed below with its corresponding number in the concordance. These inscriptions, which do not seem to conform to the hypothesis that ' , " , and ⟩ cause ⋈ , ⊗ , ✗ , ⟩ to be in the initial position, will be analyzed and explained below.

With the introduction of the "single and double" quotation signs, we must also discuss the sign . The reason for this is that the "diamond" sign, ◇ , does not occur in pairwise combination with or ◈, but it does occur often with the "double quotation."

Let us now discuss those inscriptions that do not conform to the hypothesis that signs ' , " and ⟩ cause ⋈ , ⊗ , ✗ , ⟩ to be placed in the initial position. There are a number of reasons why a prefix (consisting of a variable and a constant sign) does not seem to occur in the initial position. The most obvious explanation, though the least frequent, is the presence of multiple units of information in a single inscription. These are listed in the chart below.

A second reason why a paired prefix does not seem to be in the initial position is that the variable element of the prefix is itself a pair or polygram rather than a single sign. An example may prove helpful here. As presented in the earlier model, a prefix consists of a constant and a variable sign:

Constant Sign + Variable Sign = Prefix

⟩   ⋈   ⟩⋈

---

[42] Mahadevan, Concordance, 314.

Below is an example of a polygramic prefix:

Constant Sign + Variable Signs = Prefix

リ   ⋉ 𐤟 ∞   リ⋉𐤟∞

In these examples, the constant sign and the variable sign are single signs that form a pair when combined. However, if the variable element of the prefix consists of multiple signs, it would appear that what is thought to be a paired prefix (only two signs) occurs medially. This however is not the case, for constant signs may also cause *multiple* signs, in addition to single signs, to be placed in the initial position. This being stated, more inscriptions from the lists in the above charts can be explained. They are listed below:

	The ⊕ Sign		The ⋉ Sign
2069	𐤟 𐤟 𐤟 𐤟 𐤟 ⊙⊙⊕𐤟⊕	1027	𐤟 𐤟 𐤟 𐤟 𐤟 リ⋉
1337	' ⊕ 𐤟 𐤟 𐤟 ▦	2406	𐤟 ⊕ ‖ 𐤟 リ⋉ 𐤟 ∞
3067	𐤟 𐤟 ' ⊕ 𐤟 𐤟 𐤟		The 𐤟 Sign
2029	𐤟 𐤟 𐤟 𐤟 ' ⊕⊕	2617	‖𐤟	‖‖𐤟 𐤟 ' 𐤟
2463	𐤟 ⊙ " ⊕ ‖‖	4349	𐤟 𐤟 𐤟 𐤟 𐤟 " 𐤟 (damaged)
8029	𐤟 𐤟𐤟 " ⊕ ‖‖	7236	" 𐤟 𐤟
2130	𐤟 𐤟 ‖" ⊕ ' 𐤟	7219	" 𐤟 𐤟 (damaged)
2559	" ⊕)((damaged)	3110	𐤟 𐤟 ‖‖𐤟 ⊙ " 𐤟 𐤟
2208	𐤟 ‖‖𐤟 𐤟 " ⊕ 𐤟	7258	𐤟 𐤟 目 " 𐤟 𐤟
3155	" ⊕ 𐤟 ∷∷	7251	" 𐤟 𐤟 (damaged)
2286	𐤟 𐤟	" ⊕ 𐤟	6230	𐤟 ∷∷ " 𐤟 𐤟
2447	𐤟 𐤟 𐤟 𐤟‖" ⊕ 𐤟		The ⊗ Sign
5325	'' ⊕ (damaged)	2016	𐤟 リ ⊗ ⴹⴹ 𐤟
		3221	リ⊗𐤟 (damaged)

Figure 7: Polygramic Prefixes

Inscription #	Inscription	The Separate Units of Information
1321	𐤃𐤀𐤍𐤉𐤋	𐤃𐤀𐤍𐤉
		𐤕𐤋𐤋𐤃𐤉𐤋
2398	𐤃𐤀𐤍𐤉𐤋𐤕𐤋𐤋𐤃𐤉𐤋	𐤃𐤀𐤍𐤉
		𐤕𐤋𐤋𐤃𐤉𐤋
2690	𐤃𐤏𐤍𐤉 𐤃𐤍𐤉𐤋𐤊𐤍	𐤃𐤏𐤍𐤉
		𐤃𐤍𐤉𐤋𐤊𐤍
1012	𐤃𐤏 𐤍𐤉 𐤃𐤍𐤉𐤋𐤊𐤍	𐤃𐤏𐤍𐤉
		𐤃𐤍𐤉𐤋𐤊𐤍

Figure 8: Prefixes in Medial Position due to Multiple Units of Information on one Inscription

All of the prefixes discussed in this section have included the following five signs: ⊕, Ϗ,), ※ and ⬦. These five signs, chosen due to their high frequency, were used in this study to determine the function of ' , " and '⟩. Now that the function of these signs is known, one may now turn to inscriptions which exhibit a known constant element of the prefix, but which have less common variable signs. In other words, it has been shown that ' , " , and '⟩ cause signs ⊕ , Ϗ ,) , and ※ to be placed in the initial position. Thus one may infer that ' ," , and '⟩ can be used to determine the function of other, relatively less frequent variable signs. Let us look at some pairwise and polygram combinations other than those including Ϗ ,) , ⊕ , ※ , and ⬦ .

Inscription #	Inscription	Isolated Prefix
2632	𐤃𐤎𐤔𐤏‖"𐤅𐤃)	"𐤅𐤃)
3089	𐤃𐤀𐤎𐤃"𐤋𐤊𐤙	"𐤋𐤊𐤙
7074	𐤁𐤎"𐤀 ⫶	"𐤀 ⫶

Figure 9: Inscriptions Showing Signs Caused to be Prefixed by

Inscription #	Inscription	Isolated Prefix
4008	)𐤆※'𐤉𐤊	'𐤉𐤊
9846	⦀𐤁'𐤏𐤅	'𐤏𐤅
4630	𐤃𐤋'𐤐⬦𐤙	'𐤐⬦𐤙

Figure 10: Inscriptions Showing Signs Caused to be Prefixed by '

Inscription #	Inscription	Isolated Prefix
2264	ꓱꓯꓲꓳꓔ	ꓲꓓꓔ
3113	ꓝꓮꓲꓘ	ꓲꓘ
4139	ꓱꓥꓷꓲꓳ	ꓲꓳ

Figure 11: Inscriptions Showing Signs Caused to be Prefixed by ꓲ

It is unclear whether these prefixes represent a single unit of information or various combinations of single signs, pairwise combinations, and polygrams. It suffices to say that ' , " , and ꓲ can cause multiple signs to assume the initial position.

2.2 Terminals

It will be shown that terminal signs exhibit a hierarchical linear order. Iravatham Mahadevan, in his essay "Terminal Ideograms in the Indus Script,"[43] suggests that the following signs are terminals ꓮ , ꓮ , ꓮ , ꓵ , ꓱ , ꓐ . These signs have also been used in this study as terminals. To ꓰ these I have added the so-called "banyan" sign, ꓵꓵ , as a "variable terminal."[44] This will be discussed in greater detail below. Using these terminals as a starting point, I will further delineate a linear order to the terminals by frequency and syntax. It is well to reiterate that the purpose of the present study is restricted to the positional-statistical realm and hence the meanings attached to these signs by Mahadevan will not be assumed here.

A second scholar worth mentioning is Walter Fairservis. In his work entitled The Harappan Civilization and Its Writing System, Fairservis presents a grid which posited a linear order to the script.[45] His chart differs from the one proposed here in one basic respect. Fairservis lists the inscriptions *individually* rather than using pairwise combinations to determine order. The benefit of employing pairwise combinations is that *all* the inscriptions containing the signs in question are accounted for, while the former approach only analyzes a select number of inscriptions and omits those

---

[43] Mahadevan, "Terminal Ideograms in the Indus Script" in *Harappan Civilization: A Contemporary Perspective*, 315.

[44] The term "variable terminal" here refers to a sign whose placement is contingent on "constant terminals" (terminals that maintain consistent linear relative placement).

[45] Fairservis, *The Harappan Civilization and Its Writing System*, 226.

inscriptions that do not fit in the grid. Therefore arguments using the pairwise frequency of the signs avoids a biased selection of inscriptions by the researcher. However the drawback of the pairwise frequency approach is that one is restricted to a limited number of signs for analysis. In other words, rather than being able to order all the signs in a limited amount of inscriptions, as seen in Fairservis, one may order a limited number of signs in all the inscriptions.

Two other points pertaining to the Fairservis grid are worth mentioning. First, Fairservis lumps together many terminals into one positional slot. Those terminals will be further subdivided into their own slot in the grid reproduced below. Second, many signs that might be considered terminals are not accounted for in Fairservis. They however have been included in the following grid:

Terminal Combinations									Frequency
A [sign]	[sign]	[sign] [sign]	[sign]	[sign]	[sign]	B [sign]	[sign]	← TERMINALS	
[sign]	[sign]								3
[sign]			[sign]						6
[sign]	[sign]								26
[sign]		[sign]							2
[sign]					[sign]				11
[sign]				[sign]					184
	[sign]						[sign]		1
	[sign]			[sign]					8
		[sign] [sign]⁴⁶							1
		[sign]		[sign]					1
				[sign]			[sign]		110
			[sign]	[sign]					87
			[sign]			[sign]			1
				[sign]		[sign]			10
					[sign]	[sign]			8
						[sign]	[sign]		1

Figure 12: Positional Order of the Terminal Signs

---
⁴⁶ This is a variant of [sign].

Only one pairwise combination, 𝖸𝖸 𝖴𝖥 , having a frequency of 1, does not fit in the above

graph, for it is in disagreement with the linear order. This could easily happen due to scribal error;

𝖴𝖥 and 𝖸𝖸 in the suggested order occur 110 times.

As a side note, 𝖴𝖥 and 𝖸𝖸 , may be expressed in the abbreviated sign 𝖴𝖸 .[47] Notice that as

is always to the right of the jar (assuming the inscription is read from right to left), the banyan-like

fingers are on the right of the putative combined sign while the jar-like marks are on the left.

Therefore the combined sign reflects this same order within the sign itself.

Sign 🔯 could very well be placed to the right of 🔯 without causing syntactical error in the

grid. The situation of this sign to the left is simply the author's speculation about the sign's placement.

Regardless, one can imagine that its syntactical placement would not be too far away from signs

similar to it.

Variants have been used twice in this grid to clarify the placement of two signs.[48] The first of

these, 🕱 , is visible in the chart. This was used to determine that 🔯 does take right-hand side

priority over 🔯 . Using this variant offers another clue as well.

𝖴𝖥 and 𝝠 in their basic forms (not as a compound sign) never occur next to each other in the

script. With the variants as aids, the two pairwise combinations allow one to infer their hypothetical

relative placement 𝖴𝖥 𝝠 .

Variants were also used for 🕱 , since sufficient evidence in the terminals presented here was

not available to determine its placement. Therefore one must look at the variants of the sign for clues.

While the above grid shows that 🕱 is placed to the left of 𝖴𝖥 , its placement relative to 🕱 , 🔯 ,

and 🔯 is unknown. With some pairwise combinations that include variants of 🕱 the placement of

the sign may be inferred.

The chart below illustrates this order:

---

[47] Mahadevan, *Concordance*, Sign 352.

[48] I use the term "variants" here not to imply an exact denotation of the sign, but rather to infer a similar syntactical function of the sign.

Pairwise Combination		Frequency
𐎀	𐎁	11
𐎀	𐎁	3
𐎀	𐎁	1
𐎀	𐎁	4

Figure 13: Variants Used to Clarify Positional Placement

Therefore the variants of 大 indicate that it is placed to the right of 𐎀 , 𐎀 and 𐎀 .

Let us now consider the sign designated as "harrow," E . It may be placed to the left or the right of the "constant" terminal (arrow, jar). Thus it is seen in two positions in the above chart. Below these statistics are isolated for a clearer understanding.

Harrow in left position	Frequency of harrow in left position	Harrow in right position	Frequency of harrow in right position
E 𐎀	3	大 E	1
E 大	6	ꝟ E	10
E 𐎀	26	个 E	8
E 𐎀	2		
E 个	11		
E ꝟ	184		

Figure 14: Positional Frequencies of Harrow in Left and Right Position

While the great majority of the sign's positions are on the left (232 times), the nineteen occurrences to the right of a terminal signs are too numerous to discount as scribal error. Until more evidence presents itself in respect to this dual placement, E may be tentatively placed in either of the two slots to the left of ꝟ .

As mentioned above, Mahadevan and many others have pointed out that the arrow and jar signs almost certainly act as terminal endings,[49] but with only a cursory glance at the frequency list, one will see that out of a total of 1395 occurrences, the jar is listed as a medial sign 420 times.[50] This is quite misleading, for in the majority of the medial placements, is still acting as a terminal. Occurrences of double and triple terminals are one of the causes for this misleading statistic. Many of the terminals occurring on the list are often seen in conjunction with other terminals that take left-hand priority. As a result, the concordance catalogues the jar in medial position, when in fact it is simply joined with another terminal.

Sign 𝖸 occurs 118 times in the script. It is seen directly to the right of the jar sign 110 of these signs. The other eight times it is seen with other terminals. It is obvious that this sign acts as a "variable terminal." It cannot be considered a terminal because it is never the sole terminal sign on an inscription. It always occurs with another terminal and thus it receives the name "variable terminal."[51] With a cursory glance, one might want to label the "harrow" sign a variable terminal as well. The "harrow" sign, , often occurs with other terminals. However, since it also occurs as the only terminal in some lines of script, it may be considered simply a terminal.

Sign 目 and ⋈ as a pairwise combination

Let us now turn to the second class of terminals. Sign 目 and ⋈ will first be discussed.[52] To start, a positional breakdown of the individual signs will prove helpful.

Sign	目	⋈
Solo	0	2
Initial	3	36
Medial	9	49
Final	61	3
Total	73	90

Figure 15: Pairwise Frequencies of 目 and ⋈

---

[49] Mahadevan, *Concordance*, 12.

[50] Ibid., Solo frequency = 3; Initial frequency = 1; Medial frequency = 420; Terminal frequency = 971.

[51] G. R. Hunter was perhaps the first to notice the interaction of these two signs in *The Script of Mohenjodaro and its Connection with Other Scripts* (New Delhi: Munshiram Monaha Publishers Pvt. Ltd., 1993), 51.

[52] Asko Parpola has acknowledged these signs in the terminal position in his *Deciphering the Indus Script* (Cambridge: Cambridge University Press, 1994), 89.

One can state from the above information that ᕲ has a high frequency in the final position, while ᐅᐊ has a high frequency in the medial position. To continue, let us look at the breakdown of the two signs as they occur in pair.

The two signs occur in pairwise combination twenty-nine times in the script. Four of the twenty-nine times the signs, as a pair, occur alone on the inscription. On twenty-two occasions, the pair occurs in the final position while the remaining three occurrences must be explained further. These frequencies are summed up in the following grid:

Pairwise combination	Pairwise Frequency of Combination	Pairwise Frequency in the Final Position	Solo Occurrences of the Pair	Those Inscriptions to be Explained
ᕲ ᐅᐊ	29	22	4	3
LIST OF THE THREE INSCRIPTIONS TO BE EXPLAINED				
Inscription #	Inscription			
2868	ᕱ ᕲ ᐅᐊ			
4672	ᕱ ᕲ ᐅᐊ ꕯꕯꕯ ᗑ ᐅᐊ			
7031	ꗞꞏ ᕲ ᐅᐊ ꗖ ꞌꞌ ꝡ ꭙ			

Figure 16: Frequency Distribution of ᕲ and ᐅᐊ

The pairwise combinations of the two signs in question, occurring either solo or in the final position, are not in disagreement with our hypothesis that the pair is in fact a terminal. However, there are three inscriptions that need to be explained. These are listed above.

Inscriptions 2868 and 4672 can be explained easily, for the pair has the "harrow," a second terminal, appended to the end. The third inscription in question may also be explained with little difficulty. As discussed earlier in the section on prefixes, "constant signs" consistently change the positional slot of one or more signs. In this particular case, the pair has been displaced from its more frequent final positional slot to the initial position.

This pair, now known to be in the final placement in every case with the exception of the one occurrence where it is displaced by the prefixing element, can also be seen on two occasions with another well-known terminal sign— ᚒ :[53]

Terminals	Medial	Prefix
ᚼ ᚿ ᚒ	☒	" ◓

Terminals	Medial	Prefix
ᚼ ᚿ ᚒ	᚟	᚛ ✸

As one can see, the "jar" is situated to the right of the terminal pair. Hence from the above information, a positional chart can be formed (see below). Due to the low frequency of examples, the argument is statistically weaker than that pertaining to the class 1 terminals. However, on a positive note, there are no irregularities (e.g. scribal error) in the second class of terminals— and hence more consistency. Let us examine the grid:

Signs				Frequency
ᚕ	ᚼ	ᚿ	ᚒ	
ᚕ	ᚼ	ᚿ		2
	ᚼ	ᚿ	ᚒ	2

Figure 17: Positional Slots of the Second Terminal Class

Therefore the following order of the second class of terminals may be known as follows: ᚕ , ᚼ, ᚿ and ᚒ . It should be noted that ᚕ and ᚒ are the only known terminal signs to be seen with the terminal pair ᚼᚿ .

A discussion of ⋉

Let us now discuss the possibility of a third terminal class.[54] A grid illustrating its positional patterns of ⋉ is provided below.

---

[53] Mahadevan, *Concordance*, 2281 and 7069.
[54] Asko Parpola has commented on this sign in the terminal position in *Deciphering the Indus Script*, 95.

Solo	1
Initial	1
Medial	0
Final	15
Total	17[55]

As one may see, in fifteen out of the total seventeen occurrences, the "modified X," as it will be called from here on, is in the final position. This gives us one inscription, leaving the solo occurrence aside, to be investigated further.[56] It is given below:[57]

Terminal	Medial	Terminal	Prefix
ꝸ	▥	𐠌	" ⌈X⌉

The occurence of this sign in the initial position can be easily explained. As one may recall from the section on initial markers, the sign " may cause other signs and to be placed in the initial position. Therefore the ⌈X⌉ sign has had its placement altered by " . This initial placement of the sign is not an exception to the rule, but rather is in accordance with the rules of the script.

Sometimes signs with a similar pictography to that of ꝸ are confused as having the same positional function (acting as terminals). At first glance, it may be tempting to call sign ꝸ , or the similar signs ꝸ and ꝸ, "variants" of ꝸ . In the table below it can be seen clearly that ꝸ, ꝸ, and ꝸ have a different function than ꝸ :

Sign	Solo	Initial	Medial	Final	Total
ꝸ *Terminal*	3	1	420	971	1395
ꝸ	0	20	152	5	177
ꝸ	3	4	26	2	35
ꝸ	0	25	24	2	52

Figure 18: Positional Distribution of ꝸ , ꝸ , ꝸ , and ꝸ

Taking into consideration the positional order of the terminals, it is now known that the medial placements of ꝸ are due to other terminals assuming syntactical priority on the left-hand side.

---

[55] One should note that, due to the low frequency of this sign, the signs listed as questionable in the concordance have been included. This changes the total frequency from fifteen to seventeen. Hence two extra inscriptions have been included.

[56] This sign occurs once as solo sign. The reason for this solo placement is unknown. However, it might be inferred by this solo placement (though it is statistically weak) that the sign has an independent meaning rather than simply acting as a modifier to another sign.

[57] Mahadevan, *Concordance* 2257.

Hence, the above positional breakdown is quite misleading. Note that some of the medial placements of ⳇ displayed in the above table could also be acting as a terminal where more than one unit of information occurs in the line of script.

Signs ⳇ , ⳇ , and ⳇ , though having the great majority of their occurrence in the medial position, do occur on occasion in the initial and terminal position. These signs when in the final position should not be thought of as acting as terminals. Rather, they are more likely acting as medial signs without a terminal. An example using a less ambiguous sign will prove helpful.

Below is the positional breakdown of the so-called "crab" sign:

Solo	0
Initial	32
Medial	96
Final	2
Total	130

Having ninety-six occurrences in the medial position and thirty-two occurrences in the initial position, there is little doubt that ⳓ is not a terminal. Yet it does occur twice at the end of an inscription. It is most likely that the two terminal placements of this sign are due to the lack of a terminal. By the same token, the similarity of pictography should not mislead one to think that ⳇ , ⳇ and ⳇ are variants of ⳇ . Using pictographic similarity to infer a similarity in meaning is a highly speculative approach. Hypothetically, if one were to examine the Roman alphabet with this approach, one might confuse the letter "i" with an inverted exclamation mark, "!" While pictographically these two signs are quite similar, they have no relation in meaning. However were one to examine "i" and "!" by their placement in an inscription, one would discover their variance. Similarly, the placement of ⳇ , ⳇ , and ⳇ at the end of inscriptions, like the "crab," ⳓ , should be thought of as a medial sign on an inscription without a terminal.

2.3 Medial Signs

Statistical analysis shows a hierarchical order in the so-called "fish" signs. Even though the fish signs are medial signs rather than terminal signs, they use rules of relative order similar to those pertaining to the terminals. The five fish that are commonly seen with each other are ⳤ , ⳤ , ⳤ , ⳤ , and 𓆟 . By examining the frequency of pairwise signs, one can see that some of the fish signs take priority in right-hand placement in the pair. In other words, there is a rather consistent pattern where some fish signs occur before others. Studying all pairwise fish combinations of the above five signs is the first step to achieving meaningful results. These are listed below:

Pair	Pair Frequency	Pair	Pair Frequency
𓆟𓆟	44	𓆟𓆟	28
𓆟𓆟	24	𓆟𓆟	14
𓆟𓆟	11	𓆟𓆟	8
𓆟𓆟	7	𓆟𓆟	6
𓆟𓆟	5	𓆟𓆟	4
𓆟𓆟	4	𓆟𓆟	4

Figure 19: Pairwise Combinations of the "Fish"

If one were to remove the three pairwise combinations, 𓆟𓆟 , 𓆟𓆟 and 𓆟𓆟 (roughly 6% of the all pairs) one can order the remaining pairs (roughly 94%) on a positional grid:

Pairwise Combinations					Frequency
𓆟	𓆟	𓆟	𓆟	𓆟	←Fish in positional order
		𓆟		𓆟	44
𓆟				𓆟	24
𓆟		𓆟			28
		𓆟	𓆟		11
			𓆟	𓆟	14
	𓆟			𓆟	6
	𓆟	𓆟			8
𓆟	𓆟				7
	𓆟		𓆟		4

Figure 20: Positional Order of the "Fish" Signs

Those instances where three or more fish signs occur in sequence are also addressed in the above chart. For example, the sequence 𓆟,𓆟 and 𓆟 , seen on one inscription, remains in agreement with the above grid[58] Now let us turn to the pairwise combinations that do not conform to the above grid:

Pair	Frequency
𓆟𓆟	4
𓆟𓆟	4
𓆟𓆟	5

A problem in viewing only pairwise combinations is that one necessarily examines the "fish" signs apart from the context of the inscription. It should be noted that the frequencies of these three pairwise combinations (4, 4, 5) are the lowest totals of all of the pairwise frequencies of the "fish." Let us now look at the four inscriptions where the first pairwise combination in question   occurs:

Inscription #	Inscription
2054	𓆟𓆟𓆟𓆟‖"◇
4269	𓆟𓆟𓆟𓆟𓆟‖"◇𓆟◯
2034	𓆟𓆟𓆟‖" (damaged)
2019	𓆟𓆟𓆟𓆟‖"◇𓆟

Figure 21: Four Inscriptions Containing 𓆟𓆟

When one examines fish signs in their contexts, an interesting pattern occurs. In all four inscriptions above, 𓆟 and ‖ occur in pairwise combination. Let us focus on these two signs. An examination of their positional breakdown will prove helpful:

Sign	𓆟	Sign	‖
Solo	18	Solo	1
Initial	36	Initial	147
Medial	309	Medial	199
Final	18	Final	18
Total	381	Total	365
Frequency of the Pair			67

Figure 22: Positional Distribution of 𓆟 and ‖

[58] Ibid., 7220.

One notices that both of these signs exhibit a high frequency in the medial position. Moreover, the pairwise frequency comprises a significant portion of their individual frequency. Hence these signs are worth further investigation.[59] Let us examine some inscriptions to isolate the pair as a separate unit of information:[60]

Terminal	Medial	Prefix
⭧	𝔔 ∥	" ◇

If one were to remove the terminal and prefixing signs, one is left with the pair in question. Taking this into consideration along with the frequency of the pair in relation to their individual frequencies, one can infer that this is a separate unit of information. It is likely that ∥ gives qualification to 𝔔 .[61]

Granted this, another question arises: Is this pairwise combination a member of the ordered "fish" class discussed above, or is it separate from it? It can be inferred that, with the tools of strong and weak bonds, and the process of elimination, 𝔔∥ is in fact a separate idea from the other fish signs. Thus signs 𝔔 and ∥ are misleading due to their presentation outside of the larger inscription's context. *Without* taking into account that   is a separate idea, one could segment an inscription in the following way:[62]

Terminal	Medial	Medial	Medial	Prefix
ꙥᚲ	⋀⋀ᚦ	𝔔̂𝔔	∥	" ◇

However, with this pair now extricated as a pairwise combination, one can *reexamine* this inscription and segment it in the following way:

---

[59] Note that the initial and final occurrences are due to the lack of a prefix or terminal respectively.
[60] Ibid., 1551.
[61] Other signs may be seen that are modified by ∥ (e.g. ∥ ⊙).
[62] Ibid., 2054.

Terminal	Medial	Medial	Medial	Prefix
〤	⋀⋀	🐟	🐟‖	"◇

This being stated, 🐟 and ‖ in pairwise combination should not be included in the positional grid. The remaining two non-conforming pairs present a greater problem and may not be explained so easily. Below are these pairwise combinations in their original context:

Pair 🐟𝕏 :		Pair 🐟𝕏 :	
Inscription #	Inscription	Inscription #	Inscription
1320	〤 🐟 🐟 𝕏	3074	🔱 🐟 𝕏 🐟
3016	🔱 ‖‖ ⊌ 𝕏 〤 ⚡	2578	〤 ⬭ 🐟 𝕏 "⊛
4250	〤 𝕏 🐟 𝕏 "🐟 (damaged)	1155	〤 🐟 𝕏 〤 ⅂
4467	大 〤 🐟 𝕏	1088	🔱 🐟 𝕏 ⊕ "⊛
		4005	〤𝕏⌇🧍⊕🐟𝕏🐟"◇

Figure 23: "Fish" Pairs Not Conforming to the Positional Grid

There are no pairwise combinations, such as the one above, that would cause the pairs to be misrepresented. Hence they must be taken at face value and so remain in disagreement with the proposed positional chart.

Another interesting question can be asked: Was there geographic and temporal variation in the Indus inscriptions? While it is still not possible, given the available concordances and excavation reports, to organize the inscriptions stratigraphically, it is interesting to think about a possible cultural variation here.[63]

---

[63] Recent work by Jonathan Mark Kenoyer and Richard Meadow in the Harappa Archaeological Research Project shows that, contrary to the previous understanding of the script as having a rather static evolution, the Indus script was not so uniform in its development. They suggest, based on the stratigraphy of the archaeological record, that the Indus script had two phases. The beginning phase exhibits the animal carvings as "more angular than the later seals and the script is more curving. In later seals animal motifs tend to be more rounded while the script becomes very ridged and geometrically carved" (Jonathan Mark Kenoyer and Richard H. Meadow, "The Early Indus Script at Harappa: Origins and Development," in *Intercultural Relations Between South and Southwest Asia: Studies in Commemoration of E.C.L. During Caspers [1934-1996],* eds. E. Olijdam and R.H. Spoor [Bar International Series, in press]). I would like to thank Jonathan Mark Kenoyer for sharing this unpublished article with me. For further information on the context and dating of the script, in particular the steatite seals, see their article "The 'Tiny Steatite Seals' (Incised Steatite Tablets) of Harappa: Some Observations on Their Context and Dating," in *South Asian Archaeology: Proceedings of the Fourteenth International Conference of the European Association of South Asian Archaeologists,* eds. Maurizio Taddei and Giuseppe De Marco (Rome: Instituto Italiano Per L'Africa E L'Oriente, 2000), 1-20.

Hence from the above information, one can conclude that a positional order to all but two pairwise combinations, 𝔤𝔵 and 𝔩𝔵 may be seen. These two pairs, exhibiting the lowest frequencies of all the pairwise combinations, together make up approximately 6% of the total. Thus 94% of the "fish" pairs can be ordered consistently. For now, the two pairs not conforming to the grid must be left aside for future investigation.

Let us now turn to signs, other than the fish, that can be segmented as separate units of information.

Pairwise combination 𝖞𝖆𝖐 '''

The above pairwise combination can be isolated as a separate unit of information. Below is a positional breakdown of the signs in question:

Sign	𝖞𝖆𝖐	Sign	'''
Solo	0	Solo	0
Initial	3	Initial	16
Medial	53	Medial	54
Final	2	Final	0
Total	58	Total	70
Frequency of the Pair		27	

Figure 24: Positional Distribution of 𝖞𝖆𝖐 and '''

The above breakdown demostrates the high occurrence of these signs in the medial position. The initial and final occurrences of the signs can easily be explained by the absence of prefixes and terminals. Also, the frequency of the pair (being twenty-seven) is a significant portion of the total individual frequencies of fifty-eight and seventy respectively. Therefore the pair merits further investigation.

As one might recall from the section on the use of frequency and syntax earlier in this thesis, there are a number of ways to extricate a unit of information: 1) Pairwise combinations; 2) Strong and weak bonds; and 3) Process of elimination. Let us now apply these methods:

Individual frequency	1395	35	58	70
Inscription #1703	ꊓ	🐝	ᵥ⋀ᵥ	‖‖
Pairwise frequency		16	3	27

Firstly, the bond between the "jar," ꊓ , and 🐝 is of little value, for it represents a combination of signs from a terminal and medial class. Therefore the first combination frequency of sixteen may be disregarded. This leaves us with a combination of three and twenty-seven. One may see that the joint between ᵥ⋀ᵥ and ‖‖ (27) is stronger than the joint between 🐝 and ᵥ⋀ᵥ (3). Hence the joint of ᵥ⋀ᵥ and ‖‖ is worthy of further investigation.

The isolation of the above pair can be corroborated by a process of elimination. This is demonstrated in the following inscription:[64]

Terminal	Medial	Prefix
ꊓ	ᵥ⋀ᵥ ‖‖	"⊗

For the above inscription, one can simply remove the prefix and the terminal for   and   to be isolated as a pair. Therefore, with the use of strong and weak bonds in addition to the process of elimination one can isolate the pair.

Pairwise Combination ✳ ⵜⵜ

First let us examine the positional breakdown of the signs:

Sign	✳	Sign	ⵜⵜ
Solo	0	Solo	0
Initial	2	Initial	37
Medial	103	Medial	92
Final	0	Final	3
Total	105	Total	132
Frequency of the Pair		40	

Figure 25: Positional Distribution of ✳ and ⵜⵜ

---

[64] Mahadevan, *Concordance*, 1344.

Again, the pairwise frequency of forty is a significant portion of the individual frequencies of 105 and 132 respectively. Moreover, the two signs have a relatively high medial frequency. Using the process of elimination, one may further isolate these signs as a separate idea:[65]

Terminals	Medial
E 大 ㇗F	大 屮ᵘ

The above inscription illustrates three terminals in their respective order as discussed in the section on terminals. By removing these terminals, one is left with a pairwise combination, .

Note that the above inscription is an example of a line of text without a prefix. Therefore the pair occurs in the initial position.

Another example may prove helpful:[66]

Terminal	Medial	Medial	Prefix
㇗F	大 屮ᵘ	大	"◇

Again, with the removal of the terminal, fish, and prefix, one is left with the pair in question. Thus using the pairwise frequencies as well as the process of elimination, one can isolate the above pair as a separate idea.

Pairwise combination Ψᗺ

Let us now investigate Ψ ᗺ   as a pairwise combination. Below is the positional breakdown of the individual signs:

Sign	Ψ	Sign	ᗺ
Solo	3	Solo	1
Initial	10	Initial	35
Medial	109	Medial	128
Final	90	Final	6
Total	212	Total	170
Frequency of the Pair		54	

Figure 26: Positional Distribution of Ψ and ᗺ

---

[65] Ibid., 4325.
[66] Ibid., 2048.

The reason for investigating these two signs as a pairwise combination is due to the high frequency of the pair (54) in relation to the number of the individual frequencies (212 and 170), and the high frequency in medial placements of the two signs. To give support to this argument, let us examine the strength of the bonds of the following inscription:

Individual Frequency: (Terminal)   212   170   177   (Prefix)

Inscription #2609:

Pairwise Frequency: 54   9

From the above chart one may see that the strength of the bond between Ψ and 占 is much stronger that that of 占 and ૪F . This suggests that Ψ占 is a pairwise combination.

Let us re-examine the above inscription, this time using the process of elimination:

Terminal	Medial	Medial	Prefix
	Ψ占	૪F	𝟳𝟛

Again, one can begin by removing the terminal and prefixing signs. Three signs remain. Sign ૪F was discussed earlier in this thesis as well and may also be removed. Hence with the removal of 𝟳𝟛 (variable and constant), ૪F , and , one is left with Ψ占 . Thus Ψ占 can be segmented as a separate idea.

Further examples are listed below:

Terminals	Medial
E ૪	Ψ占

Terminal	Medial	Medial	Medial	Prefix
૪F	Ψ占	𝕏𝕏𝕏	𝟳F	𝟳𝟛

Terminal	Medial	Prefix
૪F	Ψ占	"⊕

Sign ⅩⅭ

Below is the positional breakdown of ⅩⅭ .

Solo	0
Initial	32
Medial	96
Final	2
Total	130

As one can see, the above sign has a high frequency in the medial position. As remarked above, the initial and final occurrences of the sign are not a problem. This is simply due to the absence of a prefix or terminal, which causes a medial sign to occur in the initial or final position.

First it is helpful to look at the strength of the bonds. This is exemplified below:

Individual Frequency: (Terminals) 60   70   130

Inscription #1435:   ⌐X̅¬ ƲϜ   ⋔   "⃥⃥   ⅩⅭ

Pairwise Frequency: 14   1

The weakness of the joint between "⃥⃥ and ⅩⅭ , having a value of one, suggests that   is in fact a separate idea. The process of elimination should strengthen this argument:[67]

Terminal	Medial	Prefix
ƲϜ	ⅩⅭ	" ⊗

With the removal of the terminal and the prefix signs, one is left with ⅩⅭ . From the above analysis, one can see that, through the process of elimination and the strength of bonds between individual signs, one can isolate ⅩⅭ as a separate idea.

Sign ⱷ

While in the majority of this sign's occurrences it functions as a single sign (standing as an idea by itself), it can occasionally be seen in combination with other signs to form pairwise and trigramic combinations. First let us examine an inscription where ⱷ may be functioning as a separate idea:[68]

---

[67] Ibid., 4813.
[68] Ibid., 2674.

Terminals	Medial	Prefix
全Ε	☿	"◇

By removing the two terminal signs and the prefixing sign, one is left with the sign in question, .

This is an example of a case where ☿ evidently has meaning independent of the other signs.

Yet this sign also occurs in a pairwise combination and a trigram. First let us discuss the former combination, 巛☿ . Below is a positional breakdown of the two signs:

Sign	巛	Sign	☿
Solo	0	Solo	1
Initial	2	Initial	21
Medial	35	Medial	27
Final	7	Final	5
Total	44	Total	54
Frequency of the Pair		10	

Figure 27: Positional Distribution of 巛 and ☿

Both signs appear to be similar in nature due to their relatively high frequency in the medial position. In addition, the signs occur together ten times.[69] This being stated, it is worth further investigating the two signs as functioning independently. Below is an inscription that gives insight as to whether 巛 and ☿ is in fact a pairwise combination:[70]

Terminal	Medial	Prefix
ꝛF	⊌	"巛☿

As this inscription exemplifies, this pair can be seen as a prefixing element in three of its ten occurrences.[71] The pair acting as a prefix is again suggestive of 巛☿ acting as a separate idea.

This sign may also be seen in a trigram: ᘯ△◊☿ . Let us examine at the positional information on the three signs involved in this trigram:

---

[69] Inscription numbers are as follows: 4067, 2216, 9221, 1047, 1175, 2415, 4097, 2466, 4294, 2465.
[70] Ibid., 2216.
[71] Inscription 4067, 2216 and 1047.

Sign			
Solo	0	0	1
Initial	32	3	21
Medial	96	45	27
Final	2	6	5
Total	130	54	54
Frequency of the Trigram	10		

Figure 28: Positional Distribution of  ,  and 

As one can see, the three signs that form this trigram have their highest frequency in the medial position. Moreover, the ten occurrences of the trigram is a significant relative frequency and merits the investigation of the three as functioning as a separate idea.

Let us examine some inscriptions where the autonomy of the trigram can be seen:[72]

Terminal	Medial

Terminal	Medial	Medial	Prefix

In inscription #2159 one can remove the terminal—here being a dual terminal—to isolate the trigram. Similarly, in the second inscription above one can remove the prefix, terminal, and previously isolated medial pair to see that the trigram in question is functioning as a separate idea.

Suffice it to say that, in light of the above information,  occurs in either a pairwise or trigram combination in 40% of its fifty-four occurrences (ten occurrences in  and ten occurrences in ). In the remaining thirty-three inscriptions  seems to be functioning independently—and not in combination with other signs.

Pairwise Combination 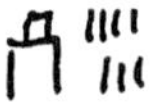

Below is the positional information of  and  :

[72] Ibid., 2195 and 1322 respectively.

Sign	⚎	Sign	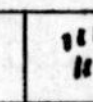 ⫴⫼
Solo	1	Solo	0
Initial	22	Initial	16
Medial	36	Medial	54
Final	1	Final	0
Total	60	Total	70
Frequency of the Pair		14	

Figure 29: Positional Distribution of ⚎ and ⫴⫼

Again, these two signs were chosen due to their relatively high frequency in the medial position as well as their high frequency as a pair in relation to their individual frequencies.

First, let us use the process of elimination:[73]

Terminal	Medial	Prefix
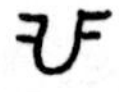 ⊅ᖴ	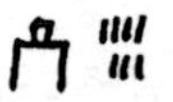 ⚎ ⫴⫼	 �ᵘ⊗

One can isolate ⚎⫴⫼ as a separate idea by removing the terminal and prefixing signs. Once ⊅ᖴ and ᵘ⊗ are removed, one is left with the pair in question, ⚎⫴⫼ . This suggests that the pair is in fact a separate idea.

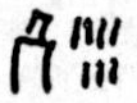

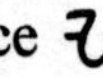

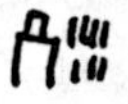

To investigate this further, let us examine the strength of the bonds in an inscription:

Individual Frequency: (Terminal)   60   70   188   130   (Prefix)

Inscription #3096:   ⊅ᖴ   ⚎   ⫴⫼   ⚔   ⌀ᗡ   ᵘᗝ

Pairwise Frequency: 14   1   4

One should note that the process of elimination as well as the strength of the bonds between the signs may be used simultaneously here. Because ⊅ᖴ, ⚔ , ⌀ᗡ, and ᵘᗝ have been isolated as separate units of information, one may isolate ⚎⫴⫼ . Additionally, one can see that the joint between ⚎⫴⫼ in relation to the individual frequencies is much greater than the joints between ⫴⫼⚔ and ⌀ᗡ⌀ᗡ . Using the above information, one can isolate ⚎⫴⫼ as a separate unit of information.

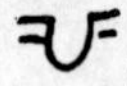

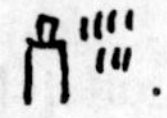

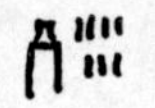

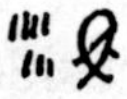

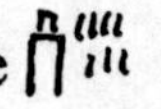

---

[73] Ibid., 2691

Sign ⚲ and ✿

Sign	⚲	Sign	✿
Solo	0	Solo	0
Initial	5	Initial	12
Medial	8	Medial	29
Final	0	Final	1
Total	13	Total	42

Figure 30: Positional Distribution of ⚲ and ✿

Signs ⚲ and ✿ were chosen for investigation as medial signs due to their relatively high frequency in the medial position. Much like the so-called "crab" sign (⊘), the above signs ⚲ and ✿ may be isolated by similar means:[74]

Terminal	Medial	Medial	Medial	Prefix
⊐F	✿	⚷⚸	⊘	'⊛

It has been demonstrated that ⊐F , ⚷⚸ , ⊘ and '⊛ are separate units of information. This indicates that ✿ is a separate unit of information as well.

The next inscription further demonstrates that ⚲ is a separate unit of information:[75]

Terminals	Medial
Ε ⊐F	⚲

The removal of the terminal signs isolates ⚲ as a separate idea.

Sign ⟨ψ⟩

Below is the positional breakdown of ⟨ψ⟩ :

Solo	0
Initial	30
Medial	72
Final	0
Total	102

While this sign does occur most frequently in the medial position, there are a significant amount of occurrences in the initial position. However, using a concordance, one can see that the great majority

---

[74] Ibid., 4016.
[75] Ibid., 4347.

of those occurrences in the initial position are simply those inscriptions without a prefix. Below are some examples of these initial occurrences:[76]

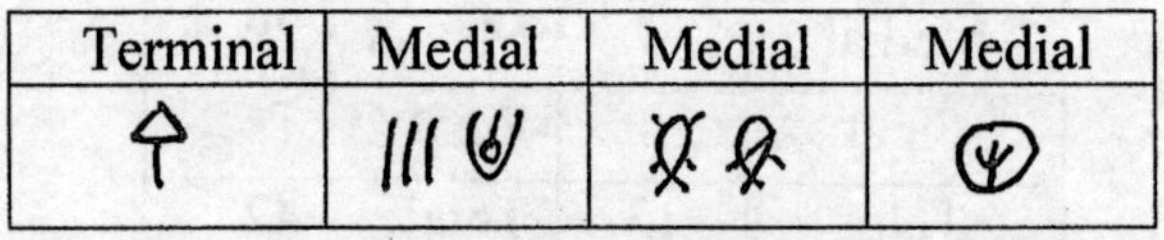
Terminal
Medial
Medial
Medial

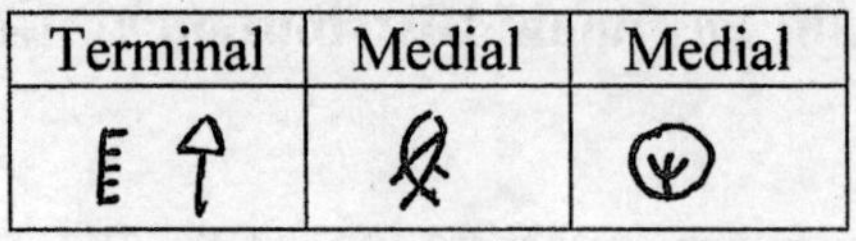
Terminal
Medial
Medial

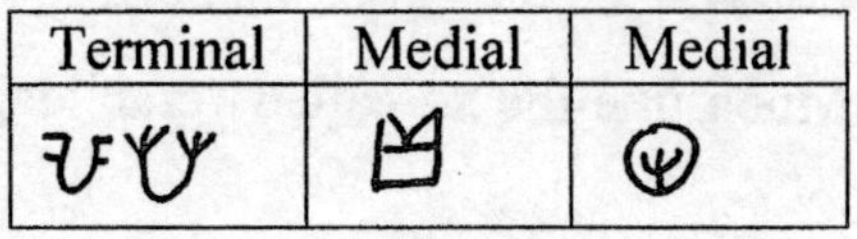
Terminal
Medial
Medial

These inscriptions, not having a prefix, can then be compared with those that do have a prefix:[77]

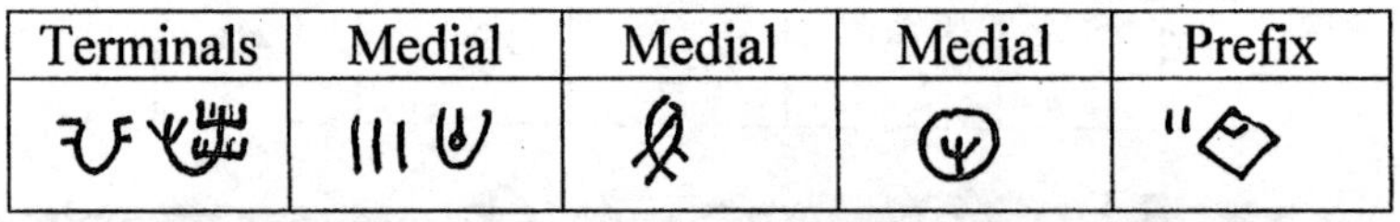
Terminals
Medial
Medial
Medial
Prefix

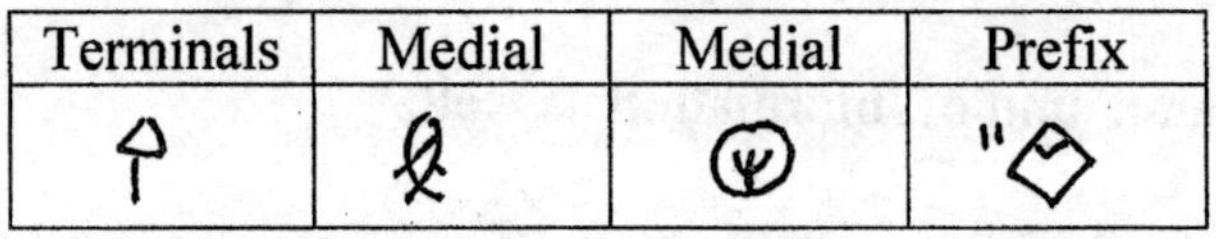
Terminals
Medial
Medial
Prefix

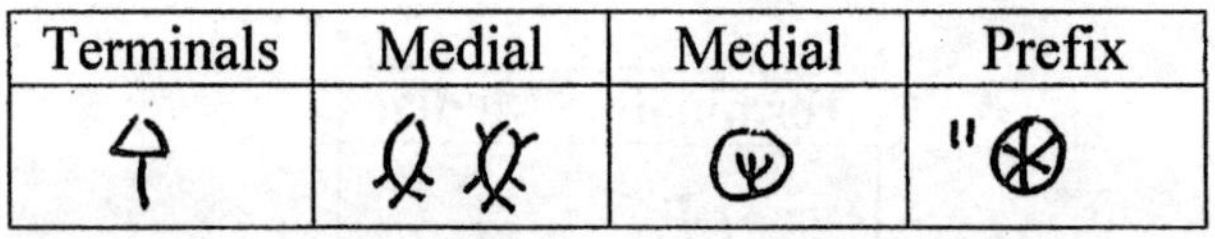
Terminals
Medial
Medial
Prefix

Hence one can then conclude that the high frequency of initial placements of  is due to the absence of a prefix.

Let us now examine some inscriptions where  may be isolated as a separate unit of information:[78]

Terminal
Medial
Medial

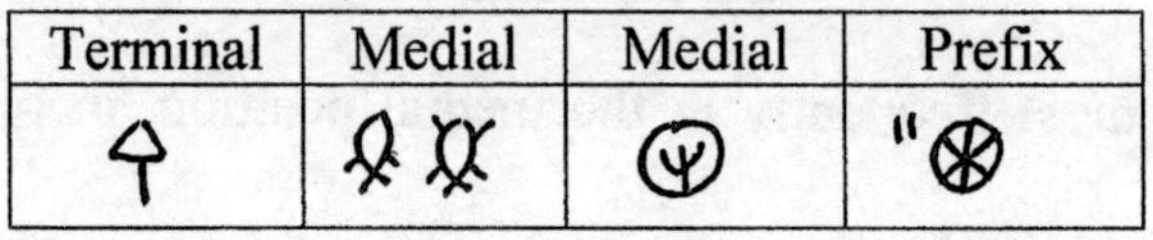
Terminal
Medial
Medial
Prefix

[76] Ibid., 2123, 1173, and 1622 respectively.
[77] Ibid., 1104, 4112, and 1088 respectively.
[78] Ibid., 3501, and 1088 respectively.

With the removal of the terminal, prefix, and other known medial signs, one can isolate the sign as a separate unit of information.

Trigram 〤〤✓〤

Let us examine the individual frequencies of the three signs that this trigram is composed of:

Sign	〤	✓	〤
Solo	2	0	1
Initial	5	0	25
Medial	65	58	75
Final	20	5	4
Total	92	63	105
Frequency of the Trigram		37	

Figure 31: Positional Distribution of 〤 , ✓ and 〤

Much like the pairwise combinations, the individual signs that compose this trigram have a high frequency of medial placements. Moreover, the frequency of the trigram, being thirty-seven, is a significant value when compared to the individual sign frequencies of the signs forming the trigram.

The process of elimination may further verify that 〤✓〤 is a separate unit of information. Let us examine the following inscriptions:[79]

Terminal	Medial	Prefix
ꓱꓞ	〤✓〤	"◇

With the removal of the terminal and prefix signs, one is left with the trigram in question.

Below is a slightly more complex inscription that supports the idea that the trigram is in fact a separate unit of information:[80]

Terminal	Medial	Medial	Medial	Prefix
ꓱꓞ	〤✓〤	⊕	〤〤〤	"◇

Knowing that ꓱꓞ , ⊕ , 〤〤〤 , and "◇ are separate units of information allows us to infer that 〤✓〤 is also a separate unit of information.

[79] Ibid., 2424.
[80] Ibid., 4005.

Pairwise Combination △△△ ϕ

To isolate △△△ ϕ as a separate unit of information, let us look at the positional breakdown of the two signs:

Sign	△△△	Sign	ϕ
Solo	0	Solo	0
Initial	3	Initial	10
Medial	45	Medial	9
Final	6	Final	2
Total	54	Total	21

Figure 32: Positional Distribution of △△△ and ϕ

Much like Ⓨ , the high frequency of △△△ ϕ in the initial position can be explained by the absence of a prefix. Let us apply the process of elimination to isolate △△△ ϕ as a separate idea:[81]

Terminal	Medial	Medial	Medial	Prefix
ⵣϜ	△△△ϕ	𝕣	𝕣‖	"◇

Terminal	Medial
ⵣϜ	△△△ ϕ

Again, with the removal of the terminal, prefix and other known medial signs,   may be isolated as a separate idea. To further corroborate this argument, the pair may be seen in isolation on the following inscription: [82]

Medial
△△△ ϕ

From this, one can conclude that △△△ ϕ is a separate unit of information.

---

[81] Ibid. 2054 and 1201 respectively.
[82] Ibid., 5304.

Pairwise Combination 𐤉𐤀

Below is the positional breakdown of 𐤉𐤀 :

Sign		Sign	
Solo	1	Solo	1
Initial	3	Initial	35
Medial	106	Medial	128
Final	130	Final	6
Total	240	Total	170
Frequency of the Pair		47	

Figure 33: Positional Distribution of 𐤉 and 𐤀

These signs were chosen as a separate unit of information due to the high pairwise frequency in relation to the frequencies of the individual signs. The process of elimination may supply additional insights to isolating the pair:[83]

Terminal	Medial
𐤆𐤅	𐤉𐤀

Terminal	Medial	Medial	Prefix
𐤆𐤅	𐤉𐤀	𐤆𐤅	𐤅𐤃

Terminals	Medial	Medial
𐤋𐤅	𐤉𐤀	𐤒

Again, with the removal of the terminals, prefixes, and known medial signs, one is left with the isolated pair 𐤉𐤀 .

Sign 𐤋 and 𐤒

Due to their positional and pictographic similarities, signs 𐤋 and 𐤒 will be examined together. I do not mean to imply by examining these signs together that they share the same meaning, for the following seal exhibits both signs on the same inscription.[84]

---

[83] Ibid., 5404, 7405 and 5276 respectively.

Terminals	Medial	Medial	Medial
巨𝒰	✳	⤳	⤳

Hence it is not likely that one is simply a graphic variant of the other. However one can speculate that they share a similar meaning.

A positional breakdown of the two signs will prove helpful.

Sign	⤳		Sign	⤳
Solo	0		Solo	1
Initial	74		Initial	5
Medial	193		Medial	10
Final	1		Final	0
Total	168		Total	16

Figure 34: Frequencies of ⤳ and ⤳

Let us begin with ⤳ . Like many previously discussed signs in this section, one can isolate ⤳ as a separate unit of information. Let us look at some examples below:[85]

Terminal	Medial	Medial	Prefix
𝒰	⤳	✳	"◇

Terminals	Medial	Prefix
大𝒰	⤳	"◇

Terminals	Medial	Prefix
=𝒰	⤳	〃✳

It is apparent that, with the removal of the prefixes, terminals and other medial information, ⤳ , can be isolated as a separate idea.

With the same method of analysis, one can also isolate ⤳ as a separate idea. Below are some examples that exemplify this autonomy.[86]

---

[84] Ibid., 5263.
[85] Ibid., 3121, 2177 and 4110 respectively.
[86] Ibid., 2379 and 1107 respectively.

Terminal	Medial
⇧	∿

Terminal	Medial	Medial	Medial	Medial
⊋Ϝ	⊙⊂	⊀	⊋Ϝ	∿

Thus it can be stated that ∿ , in addition to ⊀ , is a separate idea.

Sign ⊌ and ⊞

Below are the positional frequencies of ⊌ and ⊞ :

Sign	⊌
Solo	0
Initial	2
Medial	19
Final	0
Total	21

Sign	⊞
Solo	0
Initial	2
Medial	23
Final	0
Total	25

Figure 35: Frequencies of ⊌ and ⊞

On the basis of positional and pictographic similarity, the above two signs will be discussed together.

Let us first examine ⊌ . Some examples that demonstrate the autonomy of ⊌ are listed below:[87]

Terminals	Medial	Medial	Prefix
⊋Ϝ⋎Ⴘ	⊌	⊀‖	‖⬦

Terminal	Medial	Medial	Prefix
⊋Ϝ	⊌	⊀	‖⬦

Terminals	Medial
⊋Ϝ ⋎Ⴘ	⊌

The removal of prefixes, terminals and previously isolated medial signs demonstrates the autonomy of ⊌ .

---

[87] Ibid., 3164, 1328, and 5031 respectively.

Again the technique of isolation can also be applied to 𝕄 to yield a similar result.[88]

Terminal	Medial	Medial	Medial	Prefix
⊐Ϝ	𝕄	𝕄	⊐Ϝ	𝟄ϑ

Therefore it can be stated that ⊔ and 𝕄 are separate units of information.

Sign ⟁ and ⟁⟁

Sign	⟁		Sign	⟁⟁
Solo	0		Solo	0
Initial	3		Initial	5
Medial	31		Medial	10
Final	1		Final	0
Total	35		Total	15

Figure 36: Frequencies of ⟁ and ⟁⟁

Sign ⟁ and ⟁⟁ will be discussed together due to their relatively high frequency in the medial position as well as their similar pictography. It can be known that, while they may share similar meaning, the graphic additions to the latter sign clearly denotes a meaning separate from ⟁. This can be known by the occurrence of both signs on one inscription. It is listed below: [89]

Terminal	Medial	Medial	Medial	Medial
⊐Ϝ	)	⟁	⟁⟁	)

The following inscriptions, exhibiting signs ⟁ and ⟁⟁ , can be used in the process of elimination.[90]

Terminal	Medial
⊐Ϝ	⟁

Terminal	Medial	Medial	Prefix
⊐Ϝ	⟁	⟲	"⟁

---

[88] Ibid., 1140.

[89] Ibid., 4188.

[90] Ibid., 2360, 4057, and 1140 respectively.

Terminal	Medial	Medial	Medial	Prefix
ꝟ	𝕸	⬦⬦	ꝟ	𝄁𝄁

Hence the removal of prefixes, terminals and other previously extricated medial signs isolate ⟑ and ⟑ as separate ideas.

Pairwise Combination ||| ⊌

One can infer by positional analysis that signs ||| and ⊌ form a pairwise combination. Let us look the individual positional patterns of the two signs:

Sign	|||	Sign	⊌
Solo	7	Solo	1
Initial	71	Initial	65
Medial	70	Medial	168
Final	3	Final	2
Total	151	Total	236
Frequency of the Pair	126		

Figure 37: Positional Distribution of ||| and ⊌ [91]

A pairwise frequency of 126 is a significant value of the individual's signs total frequency. Hence ||| and ⊌ as a separate unit of information merit further investigation. The inscriptions below demonstrate this autonomy.[92]

Terminal	Medial	Medial	Medial	Prefix
⇑	||| ⊌	⚡	⊂	𝄁𝄁 ⬦

Terminals	Medial	Medial	Prefix
目 𝕏	||| ⊌	ℛ	𝄁𝄁 ⬦

Terminal	Medial	Medial	Medial
ꝟ	𝚼𝗱	||| ⊌	ℛ

Again with the removal of prefixes, terminals and other previously extricated signs, one can infer that is likely to be a separate unit of information.

---

[91] Note that the pairs | ⊌ and || ⊌ have no occurrences in Mahadevan's concordance.
[92] Ibid., 6207, 1456, and 3239 respectively.

Pairwise Combination ⚊⚊⚊ ⚊

With a positional analysis of signs ⚊⚊⚊ and ⚊ , one can conclude that the pair ⚊⚊⚊ is

likely to be a separate unit of information. Below is the positional breakdown of the individual signs:

Sign	⚊⚊⚊	Sign	⚊
Solo	0	Solo	0
Initial	3	Initial	50
Medial	45	Medial	25
Final	6	Final	1
Total	54	Total	76
Frequency of the Pair	12		

Figure 38: Positional Distribution of ||| and ⎰⎱

One might state that the pairwise frequency of twelve is not a significant enough value of fifty-six or

seventy-six to further investigate. However one might recall that ⚊⚊⚊ forms a number of other

pairwise combinations (e.g. ⚊⚊⚊ and ⚊⚊⚊). Taking these pairs into account, the frequency of

12 becomes much more significant. Hence an examination of ⚊⚊⚊ ⚊ as a pair is listed below:[93]

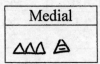

Terminal	Medial
⎍	⚊⚊⚊ ⚊

Terminal	Medial	Prefix
⎍	⚊⚊⚊ ⚊	" ⬦

Medial
⚊⚊⚊ ⚊

With the removal of prefixes and terminals, the pair ⚊⚊⚊ ⚊ can be isolated.

There are a number of signs that, based on their pictography, could be interpreted as numerals.

It is understood that there is an inherent problem with the word "numeral" when engaged in a

positional-statistical discussion, where meaning is avoided. To assign a quantitative value to a sign is

---

[93] Ibid., 2499, 2680, and 4824.

to attach meaning to it. This discrimination, based on pictography, has been done more for reference purposes. It is good to note that the division of the columns into "longer slashes, shorter slashes, and stacked slashes" has been done so that the signs are much more manageable. This division may or may not be arbitrary.

The numeral signs are some of the most challenging signs to study. All of these signs are quite simple in form; hence it is difficult to determine which of these should be thought of as variations of the same sign and which are not. Again we encounter a drawback to the exclusive use of a concordance. Ambiguous inscriptions are presented as neatly divided in the concordance. Hence there is the possibility that many signs have mistakenly placed in the incorrect column. Mahadevan explains his method for inscriptional segmentation in the concordance:

> In doubtful cases the question about sign boundaries can usually be resolved by a comparison of pairwise frequencies of signs. This can be illustrated by an example. The possible alternative readings for 1218 can be as follows:
>
> Reading A: 双 ǀ 大 ǀ ǀ   as 5 signs
> Reading B: 双 ǀ 大 ǁ   as 4 signs
> Reading C: 双 ǀ大ǀ ǀ   as 3 signs
>
> From the statistics of pairwise frequencies…it will be seen that reading C is the only tenable one as the other pairwise combinations listed above do not occur in the *Texts* (except for one doubtful occurrence of 双 in 2124).[94]

Below is a breakdown of the "numeral" signs. The grid below is quite similar to the one presented by Walter Fairservis in his "The Harappan Civilization According to Its Writing."[95] They differ mainly in that the signs and frequencies in this grid have been taken from Mahadevan.

Let us look at the various arrangements of these "slashes":

---

[94] Mahadevan, , *Concordance*, 17.
[95] Fairservis, *The Harappan Civilization According to Its Writing*, 62.

Number of Slashes	Longer Slashes	Frequency	Shorter Slashes	Frequency	Stacked Slashes	Frequency	Total Frequencies
1	|	149	'	179	N/A	-	328
2	||	365	''	678	⦙	1	1043
3	|||	314	'''	151	⦙⦙	30	495
4	||||	64	''''	70	⦙⦙	2	136
5	|||||	22	'''''	38	⦙⦙⦙	6	66
6	N/A	-	''''''	3	⦙⦙⦙	38	41
7	N/A	-	'''''''	6	⦙⦙⦙	70	76
8	N/A	-	N/A	-	⦙⦙⦙	7	7
9	N/A	-	'''''''''	1	⦙⦙⦙	2	3
10	N/A	-	N/A	-	⦙⦙⦙	1	1
11	N/A	-	N/A	-	N/A	-	-
12	N/A	-	N/A	-	⦙⦙⦙	70	70

Figure 39: Possible Numeral Signs and Their Frequencies[96]

There are number of difficulties with the above grid. As I have discussed in the section on prefixing signs, ' and '' are not likely to be numerals but rather elements in a prefix. This would significantly reduce the total frequency of the 1 and 2 slash category.

One may further reduce the total frequency of the "two-slash" row by taking into account the pairwise combination \|\| . This combination, discussed under the section on "fish" signs, is suggestive that \|\| gives qualification to ⟨ rather than acting as a separate idea. However, one may not simply subtract the amount of occurrences where \|\| is seen with ⟨ to calibrate this total. Many times \|\| is seen with signs that have a low frequency of occurrence. The number above the signs represents the individual frequency while the number below represents frequency of the pairwise combination. Frequencies have not been listed for the prefix and terminal elements, since their pairwise frequencies are irrelevant:

---

[96] The frequencies of signs '' and '' as well as ' and ' have been combined in this grid. The reason for this is that they both serve as "constant" elements in the prefix. This is discussed in greater detail in the section on "prefixes."

$$35 \quad\quad 365$$

|| [97]

5

Due to the low frequency of the majority of signs in the Indus inscriptions, it is difficult to differentiate those signs that are in pairwise combination from those where   is acting independently. The strength between bonds is helpful in determining which signs are likely to be separate ideas; however, it tells us little for determining which signs are *not* in pairwise combination. In other words, the use of the strength of bonds is helpful only when the bond is strong. Weak bonds are only useful in relation to other stronger bonds. Hence it is difficult to determine whether or not the above pair, ⌖ ||, having a pairwise frequency of five, can be considered a pairwise combination.

Therefore, as stated above, there are many ambiguous inscriptions, in respect to their frequencies, that cannot be taken into account for callibrating the frequencies in the grid totals. For now it can only be said that these totals in the one, two-slash category have been inflated due to this problem.

If one were to lump together all of the varied ways to write a "number" (short, long, and stacked), it appears that there is a significant decline in frequency after the number seven. Fairservis concluded from this that the Indus script had an eight-base system. This is surely plausible but by no means proven. One must then explain the seventy occurrences of ⦚ . If in fact ⦚ is functioning as a numeral in these cases, one would expect to see a sign of eleven and a greater frequency of eight, nine, and ten. It is also well to remember that inscriptions of all temporal and geographic locations are lumped together as one static sum in the concordance. Hence there could be cultural variation and stylistic transitions that remain unaccounted for here. Until more evidence presents itself, the mechanics of the numerical system will remain a mystery.

---

[97] Mahadevan, *Concordance*, 4268.

CHAPTER 3: THE MODEL APPLIED

A tentative framework for the Indus Script was proposed in the preceding sections of this study. However, there are many signs left which require investigation. Many of these signs, as stated above, occur at such low frequencies that any claim about their function remains highly speculative. The possible elucidation of such signs will have to be left until another date.

For now, we can work with what is known. A number of inscriptions are listed below which contain the signs and sign combinations discussed in the preceding sections. For heuristic purposes, the first four inscriptions discussed will be presented within a chart illustrating the model. In other words, the blanks will be filled in. After this, inscriptions exemplifying the same structure will be presented in an abbreviated form.

All of the signs in the following inscriptions have been discussed in the preceding sections. For information as to how a particular sign or group of signs has been extricated, one can refer to the index of signs contained in Appendix B. Here one will find the signs discussed in the present work and their corresponding page numbers.

The inscriptions presented below have been chosen to illustrate the hierarchical order of a group of signs (e.g. terminals, fish), to exhibit an overall structural order (prefixes and terminals), or to demonstrate text segmentation. Let us look at the first examples:

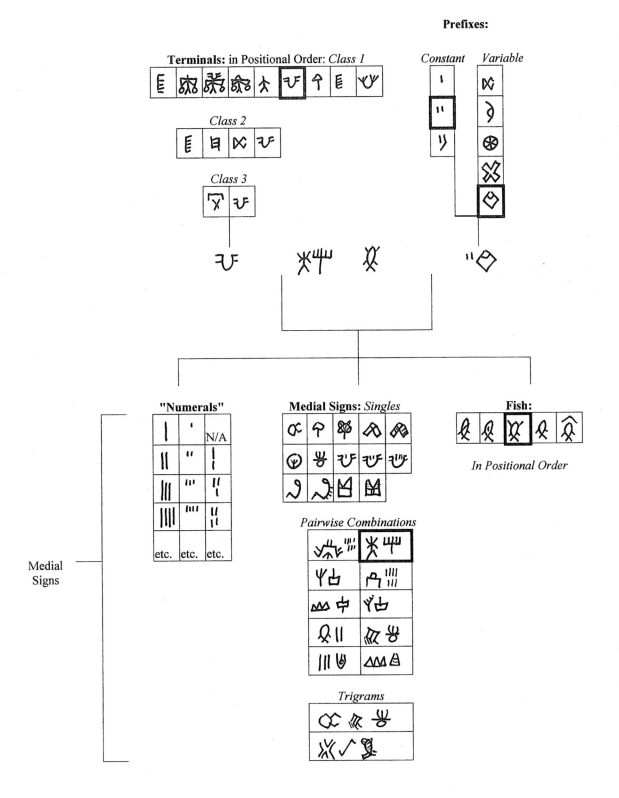

Figure 40: Inscription 2048 in Positional Chart

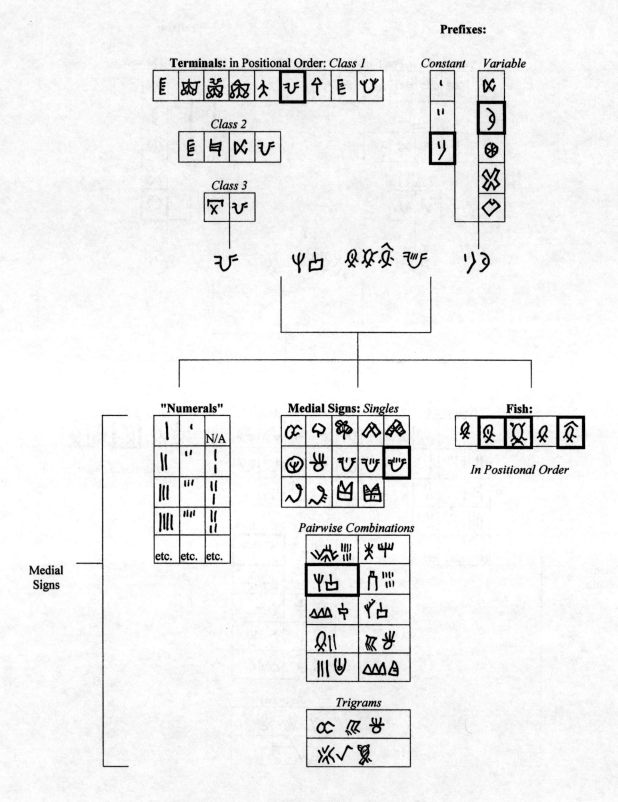

Figure 41: Inscription 4104 in Positional Chart

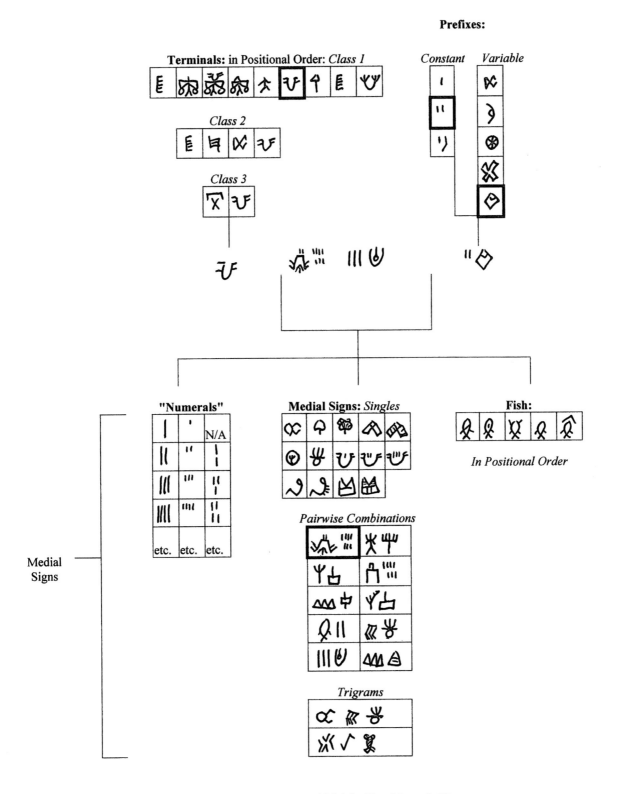

Figure 42: Inscription 4021 in Positional Chart

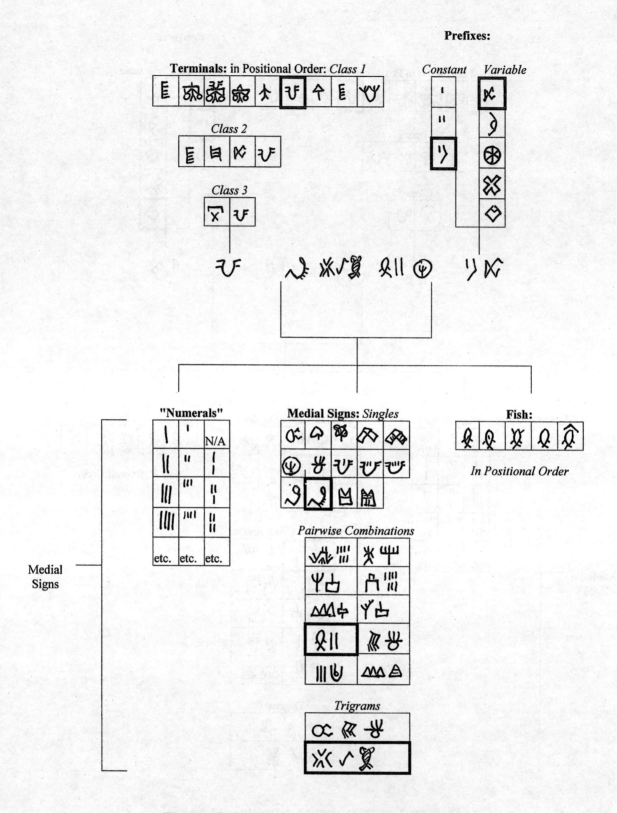

Figure 43: Inscription 4019 in Positional Chart

INSCRIPTION 2048:

This is a rather simple inscription. Its final sign (left-hand side) is, ⟨glyph⟩, the most frequent terminal. Similarly, it is prefixed with the most common pairwise combination, ⟨glyph⟩. Removing the prefix and terminal sign, one is left with the medial information: a "fish," ⟨glyph⟩, and the pairwise combination ⟨glyph⟩. Thus one can conclude that this inscription is composed of four structural parts: a prefix (variable and constant), a single medial, a pairwise medial, and a single terminal.

INSCRIPTION 4104:

The prefix in this inscription is a combination of the variable and constant elements ⟨glyph⟩ and ⟨glyph⟩. The end of the inscription (left-hand-side) has the terminal ⟨glyph⟩. The medial information consists of a medial, ⟨glyph⟩, a "fish" trigram (in their positional order ⟨glyph⟩ ⟨glyph⟩ ⟨glyph⟩), and the previously isolated pairwise combination ⟨glyph⟩.

INSCRIPTION 4021:

With an initial glance, one could suggest that the two groups of numerical signs are related due to their similarity in appearance. However, given the analysis of the present work, it is now known that the pairwise combination ⟨glyph⟩ ⟨glyph⟩ is a separate idea from the other pair ⟨glyph⟩. This inscription also has the typical prefixing and terminal elements.

INSCRIPTION 4019:

This inscription can be divided into six units of information. The first step is to remove the prefix and terminal signs (two units of information). Next one has (in right to left order) a single sign ⟨glyph⟩, a pairwise combination ⟨glyph⟩, a trigram ⟨glyph⟩, and another single sign ⟨glyph⟩ (four units). These signs have all been discussed in their respective sections in this thesis.

Below additional segmented texts are listed:

Inscription #4073:

Terminals	Medial	Medial	Prefix
🜲𐤖	Ⱥ	|||	″◇

Inscription #2338:

Terminals	Medial	Medial	Prefix
𐤁 𐤅	🜲 𐤍	𐤗	″◇

Inscription #4016:

Terminal	Medial	Medial	Medial	Prefix
𐤅	🜲	𐤀 𐤗	ↄc	ʼ⊗

Inscription #1630:

Terminal	Medial	Medial	Prefix
𐤅	🜲 𐤍	𐤅	𐤃

Inscription #2054:

Terminal	Medial	Medial	Medial	Prefix
𐤅	⋀⋀ 𐤗	𐤀	𐤀||	″◇

Inscription #2081:

Terminal	Medial	Medial	Prefix
𐤔	𐤀 𐤗	𐤅	″◇

Inscription #7009:

Terminal	Medial	Medial	Medial
𐤔	𐤀 𐤗	𐤅	″◇

Inscription #6217:

Terminal	Medial	Medial	Prefix
𐤔	𐤀	𐤅	″◇

Inscription #4666:

Terminals	Medial
(symbols)	(symbols)

Inscription #4451:

Terminals	Medial	Medial
(symbols)	(symbols)	(symbols)

Inscription #4056

Terminal	Medial	Medial	Prefix
(symbols)	(symbols)	(symbols)	(symbols)

Inscription #4005

Terminal	Medial	Medial	Medial	Prefix
(symbols)	(symbols)	(symbols)	(symbols)	(symbols)

Inscription #2541

Terminal	Medial	Medial	Medial	Medial
(symbols)	(symbols)	(symbols)	(symbols)	(symbols)

Inscription #2511

Terminals	Medial	Prefix
(symbols)	(symbols)	(symbols)

Inscription #2480

Terminal	Medial	Medial	Medial	Prefix
(symbols)	(symbols)	(symbols)	(symbols)	(symbols)

Inscriptions #1321 (also #2398)

2nd Unit of Information			1st Unit of Information		
Terminal	Medial	Prefix	Terminal	Medial	Prefix
(symbols)	(symbols)	(symbols)	(symbols)	(symbols)	(symbols)

Inscription #2690 (also #1012)

2nd Unit of Information			1st Unit of Information		
Terminal	Medial	Prefix	Terminal	Medial	Prefix
⊐∪⊏	⊕	リ ✕	⊐∪⊏	✕∧⧈	リ ✕

CHAPTER 4: AN INTERPRETATION OF THE ANALYSIS

A tentative structural model demonstrating a stability of positional slots for the signs used in the Indus inscriptions has been proposed. How then would this model affect the current understanding of Indus inscriptions? Let us first rehearse two previously suggested functions for the Indus script that can now be ruled out as possibilities in the light of the above study. These are the so-called "nominative" and the "narrative" functions.

Researchers using Dravidian models for decipherment often advocate a nominative function for the script. I am using the term "nominative function" to mean that the seals and sealings were used to identify people; for example, "John Doe the Coppersmith," or "Jane Doe from the buffalo clan." Iravatham Mahadevan, one of the most systematic and careful students of the Indus script, has been a leading supporter of this position. His contributions—such as the essential concordance of Indus inscriptions, his positional-statistical research, and critique of unscientific decipherment attempts—are quite admirable.[98] However, it is this author's opinion that sufficient evidence is available, in light of the above model, to rule out the nominative function of these seals. The argument will rely on two observations: (1) multiple units of information, though infrequent, can be found on a single inscription, and (2) inscriptions vary in length on functionally similar objects.

4.1 The Nominative and Narrative Function

In his article entitled "Study of the Indus Script through Bilingual Parallels," Mahadevan states the following in favor of the nominative function, "The Harappan seals, in accordance with universal

---

[98] Iravatham Mahadevan, "Aryan or Dravidian or Neither: A Study of Recent Attempts to Decipher the Indus Script," *Electronic Journal of Vedic Studies* 8.1 (March 2002), available from http://users.primushost.com/~india/ejvs/issues.html.

usage, give the names of their owners. The longer texts probably also contain titles, honorifics, references to occupations, place-names and other ancillary information."[99] With this premise, one would expect to see a basic title with ancillary information attached to the beginning or end of the inscription. Yet as shown in the present thesis, one can recognize the beginning and end of one unit of information given the frequency of placement of the terminals and prefixes.[100] Therefore, as discussed above, the end of an inscription can be marked with terminals while the beginning of a unit of information may be identified as a prefix. One then can segment the texts based on the presence of prefixes and/or suffixes. This being stated, one can now examine these longer inscriptions to see if their format coheres with Mahadevan's hypothesis.

The first of the longer inscriptions is worthy of analysis:[101]

1. ⟨script symbols⟩
2. ⟨script symbols⟩
3. ⟨script symbols⟩

Here is a seal that contains three lines of script on one side. The first line of script is of the common format, having ⟨symbol⟩ as a terminal. Note too that ⟨symbol⟩ often has an initial placement in a pairwise combination. Hence this line can be considered a self-contained segment. The next line of the seal begins with ⟨symbol⟩. This is its only occurrence in the corpus of seals. Hence almost nothing of significant positional value can be deduced from this sign. However, the second line of text ends with as well as its common attachment   (a variable terminal). This feature corroborates the idea that the first and second lines comprise separate units of information. The third line of script is much more difficult to analyze due to the low frequency of its signs. While more information with respect to the

---

[99] Iravatham Mahadevan, "Study of the Indus Script Through Bi-lingual Parallels," in *Ancient Cities of the Indus,* ed. Gregory Possehl (New Delhi: Vikas Publishing House, 1979), 262.
[100] Mahadevan is familiar with the separation of units of information by the medial placement of terminals. See Mahadevan, "Terminal Ideograms in the Indus Script," 311-317.
[101] Mahadevan, *Concordance*, 1400.

positional patterns of the third line would be helpful, enough information is provided by the first two lines to formulate an argument. The crux of this point revolves around the fact that two separate units (or "titles" to use Mahadevan's hypothesis) of information are on the seal. It no longer can be said that the longer inscriptions are simply titles lengthened by ancillary information. Rather, the seals, using the approach suggested by Mahadevan, must contain more than one *title*. This, in turn, produces serious theoretical problems regarding the function of the seals. Would it not be impractical to have more than one title on a seal or sealing? Furthermore, if in fact the terminal signs were class-indicating suffixes, one would see an example of two classes—if we are to take Mahadevan's idea seriously that suffixes are indicators of social class—illustrated on one seal—the first line ending in while the second ending with .[102]

To further investigate the matter, it is useful to investigate another seal exhibiting one line of script. Seal 2690 has one line of script:

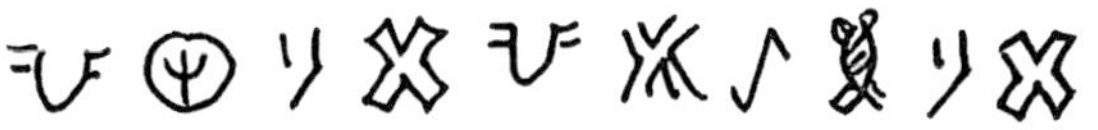 [103]

With further investigation it becomes apparent that two units of information are expressed on the seal. Notice that the initial signs and terminal signs are the same for each unit of information. The initial signs here are a pairwise combination that together form a prefix (see section 2.1 on prefixes). Again, one is faced with the same problem if the seals are to be understood as providing titles with appended auxiliary information. The two units of information here, rendered similarly, must represent two analogous units of information (two titles?) and not a title with appended auxiliary information. Again, the occurrence of numerous titles on one seal seems problematic.

If one accepts a nominative function for the inscriptions, one must make a decision: at what point in the inscription does the inscription become a title? For example, the following inscriptions exemplify the varying lengths of a seal:

---

[102] For Mahadevan's discussion on terminals as class-indicating suffixes, see his article entitled "Terminal Ideograms in the Indus Script," in *Harappan Civilization: A Contemporary Perspective* (Oxford: Oxford University Press, 1982). 311-317.
[103] Mahadevan, *Concordance*, 2690.

$$\triangle\triangle\triangle \ \underline{A} \quad {}_{104}$$

$$\triangle\triangle\triangle \ \underline{A} \quad {}_{105}$$

$$\Upsilon \ \triangle\triangle\triangle \ \underline{A} \ ^{\backprime\prime}\diamondsuit \quad {}_{106}$$

$$\exists\Upsilon \ \Psi\Upsilon \ \uparrow \ \beta \ \triangle\triangle\triangle \ \underline{A} \ ^{\prime\prime}\diamondsuit \quad {}_{107}$$

Surely the last inscription could be considered a title under the nominative hypothesis, whereas the first of these is far too simple to be considered a title (there is no terminal or prefix on the seal). One would expect the function of the seals (especially the stamp seals) would be consistent regardless of the length of the inscription. This again is evidence which suggests a re-evaluation of the nominative function of the seals.

In a "narrative" function of the script, one would expect to see sentences; for example, "Head Chief goes to the temple." Steve Farmer has quite convincingly argued that the Indus inscriptions could not have encoded speech.[108] Moreover, the nonlinguistic nature of the Indus inscriptions is corroborated in the present work by the fixed positional order of the terminals and fish signs. Redundancy will be avoided here. However let us look at some other points that pertain to the alleged narrative function.

Again, given the varying lengths of the inscriptions, one must decide: at what point in length does an inscription become a sentence? The examples in the previous section can again be used here. While an inscription with ten signs could theoretically be discursive, an inscription consisting of only one sign is not likely to serve a "narrative" function. Moreover, if there were a narrative function, one would surely expect to see longer inscriptions (that is, greater than three lines of texts) similar to those produced by their westerly neighbors.

For obvious reasons, a majority of scholars are in agreement that the Indus inscriptions did not function in this capacity. Hence a lengthy discussion on this topic is not necessary.

---

[104] Ibid., 4824.
[105] Ibid., 2499.
[106] Ibid., 2860.
[107] Ibid., 2290.
[108] Farmer, "Five Cases of 'Dubious Writing,'" handout.

4.2 The Votive and Economic Function

As stated in the introduction, the interpretation of the analysis is always more speculative than the analysis itself. This may seem tautological; however, it is necessary to emphasize this point. Many decipherers have the assumption that their analysis can only lead to one conclusion—that, of course, is their own conclusion! Therefore, it should be stated that the following observations on the possible function of the script is simply my *interpretation* of the analysis. One may only state which functional possibilities are *not* in disagreement with above analysis. Two possibilities will be discussed here—a votive/religious function and an economic function

With only a cursory glance at the stamp seals, the religious nature of the motifs is apparent. Humped zebus are adorned with jewelry; what seem to be devotees can be seen kneeling toward a person of elevated status; and of course there is the often-debated "Proto-Śiva" motif. It is not hard to conceive that the Indus inscriptions, especially those with motifs of this nature, had a religious function.

An interesting question arises here. What is the relationship between the motif and the inscription? Is an apparently religious motif indicative of a religious script? Let us say, hypothetically, that archaeologists in the future are excavating an occupational layer in the U.S. dating from the nineteenth century. In this excavation, a number of coins are discovered, all bearing what seem to be figures of devotion (the busts of the presidents). One might suggest, based on this common motif, that the coins were religious tokens of devotion. This of course would be an erroneous interpretation. Though there are arguably religious (at least at the level of civil religion) elements on the coin, its main purpose is utilitarian. Whether or not this is the case for the Indus inscriptions is another matter. It can be said that there is a danger in building assumptions about the function of the script based on the various illustrative motifs. Therefore, no inferences on the script will be made based on the motif.

The use of an economic script may be used to solve many problems of oral transactions. For example, let us say that in a local market in Harappa, Śiva sells Mahaveer fifty micro-beads in a vessel.

The transaction is then sealed with a stamp sealing. When Mahaveer returns home, he discovers that there are only forty micro-beads. The use of a sealing which recorded evidence of the transaction would allow him to confront the seller or local authorities about the problem. Thus the sealing acts as a receipt for the transaction.[109] On the other hand, let us say that no sealing was used in the transaction. This causes a much larger problem, for there is now no written record of the transaction. The seller, Śiva, could easily be dishonest and say that he sold Mahaveer only fourty microbeads.

There are a number of questions that arise. Could one not simply forge a seal? Why would one go through the effort of making a seal for the transactions? What type of information would be conveyed on a sealing being exported to another city? Would a sealing from Kalibangan containing a person's name and rank not seem irrelevant to a person from Mohenjo-Daro? What drives an individual to suffer the trouble of exporting or importing a sealing (whatever it was attached to)?

For insight into these questions, it may be helpful to look toward their westerly neighbors. Below is an excerpt from and article by Daniel Potts entitled "Distant Shores: Ancient Near Eastern Trade:"[110]

> Dilmun's particular character was expressed in economic transactions by the use of an immediately identifiable and at the same time highly decorative type of circular stamp seal. In the ancient Near East both stamp and cylinder seals were employed for the witnessing of an act, the validation of a document, the confirmation of an agreement, the identification of a party to a transaction, the certification of the accuracy of a stated quality, and the protection of an individual or institution…That these seals were used in economic transactions is proven by the discovery of two important tablets bearing their impressions. One of these tablets was found at Susa, and dates to the first half of the second millennium. It is a copper receipt for goods, including ten minas of copper. The second tablet, in the Yale Babylonian collection, is dated to the tenth year of Gungunum of Larsa…and records a consignment of goods prior to a trading voyage that almost certainly had Dilmun as its goal.

As stated above, it is surely conceivable that the Indus seals may have served a similar function. The script at the top of a seal could conceivably express the commodities, their quantity, locations, and the

---

[109] This function has previously been argued by J.V. Kinnier Wilson in *Indo-Sumerian: A New Approach to the Problems of the Indus Script* (Oxford: Clarendon Press, 1974).

[110] Daniel T. Potts, "Distant Shores: Ancient Near Eastern Trade with South Asia and Northeast Africa," in *The Civilizations of the Ancient Near East,* ed. Jack M. Sasson (New York: Macmillan, 1995), 3:1453.

proprietor etc. while the motif was "guarantor of the transaction." Hans J. Nissen also makes this

observation in reference to the Near East:[111]

> Not only does the seal impression secure the integrity of the surface of a clay document, but the individual who impressed his seal is often identified as the guarantor of the transaction involved.

Other remains in the archaeological record support this hypothesis. For example, there is evidence of

both small and large-scale workshops in Harappan cities.[112] In such workshops the same products were

continuously manufactured. Hence a person producing items in bulk would only need a few stamp

seals to stamp the entire range of items being produced.

Much as in West Asia, information could be omitted which was obvious to the consumer.

Again it is helpful to cite Nissen here:[113]

> Everything expected to be known by the reader was omitted by the scribe. Thus there was obviously no need to elaborate on syntactic relationships, for example, to include extra information about the sender or receiver of goods involved.

Let us say that a bale of barley, weighing two Harappan units, was being sold. Surely the consumer

would know by examining the bale that it was in fact barley. Hence it would not be necessary to

inscribe that information on the seal.

This statement by Nissen parallels nicely with the positional data we have been examining. As

shown in chapters two and three, inscriptions may have a combination of a number of components (i.e.

prefix, various medial information, and/or terminal). In turn, in any given inscription, some of this

information may be left off. For example, an inscription may have a prefix and no terminal while

another inscription may have a terminal and no prefix. The presence of numerical notation on some

inscriptions and its absence on others provides another example. It is certainly plausible that the

varying range of lengths of the inscriptions may reflect the omission of information that was obvious to

the consumer.

---

[111] Hans J. Nissen, *Archaic Bookkeeping: Early Writing and Techniques of Economic Administration in the Ancient Near East* (Chicago: University of Chicago Press, 1993), 15.

[112] Jonathan Mark Kenoyer, *Ancient Cities of the Indus Civilization* (Oxford: Oxford University Press, 1999).

[113] Ibid., 20.

As well as items being traded within the city, there is evidence that suggests trade to much farther geographic locations as far as Sumer.[114] One can conceive of additional characters being incorperated on those sealings stamped for export as opposed to those destined for use in the local market. One might ask: Why are there not more *sealings* in the archaeological record that reflect such economic activity? It is known that the archaeological record is severely biased in what it preserves. An argument from silence is an argument that should be avoided. The stamp *seals* that have survived were made of durable materials, like stone, bronze, and baked clay, whereas the *sealings* were impressed in unbaked clay. Taking into consideration the several thousand years that have passed since the Mature Harappan period, it is not difficult to imagine that much of the unbaked material would have decomposed. The presence of jars stamped before they were baked further exemplifies this partiality of excavated items. Moreover, truly corroborative evidence for this premise was discovered at the 'warehouse' of Lothal. Here numerous sealings were found at the port of the city where a warehouse is thought to have burned down.[115] It seems plausible to conclude that the scarcity of sealings is due to the bias of the archaeological record.

More support for the economic function of the script can be drawn from other aspects of archaeology. It is known that economic activity in the Indus region significantly increased from the Early Harappan period to the Mature Harappan period. During the Mature period, long distance trade networks became established within the pan-Indus area. Pottery styles influenced most heavily by Kot Diji and Amri phases became somewhat standardized. Standardized burnt bricks, also an adaptation from Kot Diji, became common in house and public architecture. It is intriguing that the Indus script makes a rather sudden emergence in this transition from the Early Harappan to Mature Harappan periods.

Given the above consideration, it may be said that the economic function of the script is perhaps the most likely candidate for interpreting the significance of the Indus script. A written script has the ability to solve many of the problems of oral transaction. The Harappans, who were in contact

---

[114] Potts, "Distant Shores," 452-59.
[115] Kenoyer, *Ancient Cities*, 84.

with their westerly neighbors, surely encountered the various writing systems of that area. The utility

of such as tool would surely have been appreciated.

CHAPTER 5: CONCLUSION

It would be wonderful to conclude with some dazzling results that "crack the code" to the Indus inscriptions. With the positional-statistical approach, this type of sensational result cannot be achieved. The above research is not without avail however. A small, though quite necessary, step has been made. As demonstrated in chapters two and three, we can begin to discern an order in the Indus script inscriptions. From this order we can start to speculate on its possible function.

Let us first review what, in respect to the positional-statistical aspects of the script, can be stated so far:[116]

1) Inscriptions may contain one of three major types of information: prefixes, terminals, and medial information ("numerals," "fish," and other isolated units).

2) Terminals and fish signs occur in a set linear order.

3) Prefixes are composed of a constant and variable element(s)—the constant sign causing the variable element(s) to be placed initially.

4) Prefixes, various types of medial signs, and terminals, for whatever reason, may be left off the inscription if they are not necessary.

5) Multiple units of information may occur in one inscription.

The first element that a line of text may begin with (being read from right to left) is the prefix. This is a two-part prefix, having a constant and variable component. The constant is a sign that always occurs in the initial position (second to the variable). The sign in the variable position is often a sign that, when not seen with the constant, can occur in any position (final, medial, or initial). However

---

[116] See Appendix A for the positional grid.

when in pairwise combination with the constant, the sign assumes the initial position. Prefixes also occur where more than one sign (variable signs) is put in the initial position due to the constant.

Then there are the terminals. Much like the fish signs, a positional order occurs in the terminals. There are three classes of terminals. Class one is by far the largest and most frequent while classes two and three are smaller and less frequent.

The medial information includes the majority of the signs. Within this category are the "fish" signs, "numeral signs," and other signs and combination of signs. Within the fish signs, a consistent positional order can be seen. Aside from the fish, many signs and combinations of signs may be segmented by the process of elimination and by the strength of the bonds between signs. These techniques permitted the generation of a list of extricated signs (see Appendix B). With such a list one may be better prepared for

a priori approaches, where meaning is inferred based on the pictographic transparency of a set of signs.

The segmented medial units could be useful as the first step to inferring meaning in the Indus inscriptions. While it is not likely that the language of the Harappans was a form of Dravidian, comparisons with Masica's language X and Munda (a form of Austro-Asiatic) are worthy of further investigation.[117] While such comparisons of Indus inscriptions with the oral texts of the Rig Veda (where loan words from Munda and Masica's language X are found) rely on pictographic transparency for meaning, the nature of the loan words themselves are of exceptional interest. Based on linguistic studies, it is thought that Indo-Iranian branched off from Indo-European before the development of agriculture.[118] Therefore many agriculturally related words in the Rig Veda are non-Aryan in origin. If our hypothesis that the Indus script inscriptions had an economic function is correct, one might speculate that items related to agriculture should be among the signs in the Indus inscriptions. Hence a

---

[117] Michael Witzel, "The Languages of Harappa: Early Linguistic Data and the Indus Civilization." in *Proceedings of the Conference on the Indus Civilization*, ed. Jonathan Mark Kenoyer (Madison, 1998). Provisional copy available from www.people.fas.harvard.edu/~witzel/IndusLang.pdf.

[118] One of the arguments for this theory is that words, previously not related to agriculture, were later developed to describe agricultural related items and activity in Indo-European. However, this phenomenon does not occur in the Indo-Iranian branch. Rather a number of loan words (not Aryan in origin) take their place. For an in depth discussion on this see Colin P. Masica's article entitled "Aryan and Non-Aryan in North Indian Agriculture" in *Aryan and Non-Aryan in India*, ed. Madhav M. Deshpande and Peter E. Hook, Michigan Papers on South and Southeast Asia No. 14, (Ann Arbor: The University of Michigan Center for South and Southeast Asian Studies, 1978), 55-151.

comparison among these loanwords of the Rig Veda and the pictographic transparency and segmentation of the Indus inscriptions, even though speculative, seems like a worthwhile endeavor.[119] It is my hope that the present thesis will further such research.

It should be stated that by no means do I intend this model to be thought of as set in stone. Rather, I think of the model as a necessary starting point. Certainly with the input of others and the discovery of new inscriptions, the model will require repeated refinement.

Admittedly there are drawbacks to the positional-statistical approach. This approach, in itself, gives no insight into the possible meaning of the Indus script inscriptions. One must sacrifice meaning in order to achieve objectivity in the analysis. Using linguistic presuppositions, one might be tempted to force upon the inscriptions (whether consciously or subconsciously) a structure that does not exist. Therefore I would assert it is only after an analysis of the positional patterns in the script that one may pursue meaning.

Discovering the major patterns of how the script is structured does not necessarily lead us to how the script functioned either. It was argued in chapter four that the script plausibly served an economic function. One may only argue that a hypothesis does or does not conform to the model. A functional hypothesis that conforms to the model surely does not imply that the script must have functioned that way. Instead, one may only say that a functional possibility is *not* in disagreement with the model. Hence the suggested model may simply be used as an aid to the archaeological record in respect to how the script functioned.

On a personal note, I think that the decipherment attempts in the past have attempted to grasp much more than what is knowable. For example, it is not likely that we will decipher a word such as "blue," for pictographic transparency, the only beginning point one has at this point for discovering meaning, can tell us little about abstract words. Additionally, one cannot be certain that signs, considered to be pictographically transparent, actually denote the object they are modeled after. Given

---

[119] It is noteworthy that Dravidian loanwords are present in the early books of the Rig Veda. However, it is not until the later books that they appear with significant frequency. It is thought by some that such an increase was due to the Dravidians not being autochthonous to India, but rather migrants themselves. Such a theory would explain the isolated pocket of Brahui, a Dravidian language, in the region formerly inhabited by the Harappans; see Witzel, "The Languages of Harappa."

the brevity of the Indus inscriptions, one must accept that, unlike cuneiform or hieroglyphic inscriptions, a rather dramatic unraveling of the script is not likely. Instead we can expect progress toward resolving the meaning of the Indus script to be much more gradual.

REFERENCES

Bonta, Christopher Steven. *Topics in the Study of the Indus Valley Script.* M.A. Thesis, Brigham Young University, 1996.

Daniels, Peter T. "Methods of Decipherment." In *The World's Writing Systems*, eds. Peter Daniels and William Bright, 141-59. New York: Oxford University Press, 1996.

Fairservis, Walter A. *The Harappan Civilization and its Writing: A Model for the Decipherment of the Indus Script.* New Delhi: Oxford University Press & IBH Publishing, 1992.

_____. "Harappan Civilization According to its Writing." In *South Asian Archaeology*, ed. Bridget Allchin, 154-161. Cambridge: Cambridge University Press, 1981.

Farmer, Steve. "Five Cases of 'Dubious Writing' in Indus Inscriptions: Parallels with Vinča Symbols and Cretan Hieroglyphic Seals." Handout from the Fifth Harvard Indology Roundtable, 2003. Available from http://www.safarmer.com/downloads. Accessed February 24, 2004.

Hunter, G. R. *The Script of Mohenjodaro and its Connection with Other Scripts.* New Delhi: Munshiram Monaha Publishers Pvt. Ltd., 1934.

Joshi, Jagat Pati and Asko Parpola, eds. *Corpus of Indus Seals and Inscriptions: Collections in India.* Helsinki: Suomalainen Tiedeakatemia, 1987.

Kenoyer, Jonathan Mark. *Ancient Cities of the Indus Civilization.* Oxford: Oxford University Press, 1999.

Kenoyer, Jonathan Mark and Richard H. Meadow, "The Early Indus Script at Harappa: Origins and Development." In *Intercultural Relations Between South and Southwest Asia: Studies in Commemoration of E.C.L During Caspers (1934-1996),* eds. E. Olijdam and R. H. Spoor (BAR International Series, in press).

_____. "The 'Tiny Steatite Seals' (Incised Steatite Tablets) of Harappa: Some Observations on Their Context and Dating." In *South Asian Archaeology: Proceedings of the Fourteenth International Conference of the European Association of South Asian Archaeologists*, eds. Maurizio Taddei and Giuseppe de Marco. 1:1-20. Rome: Instituto Italiano Per L'Africa E L'Oriente, 2000.

Kondratov, A.M. "The Positional-Statistical Analysis of the Proto-Indian Texts." In *The Soviet Decipherment of the Indus Valley Script: Translation and Critique.* Translated by Arlene R. K. Zide and Kamil V. Zvelebil. The Hague: Mouton & Co. B. V., 1976.

Korvink, Michael. "The Indus Script: A New Decipherment Paradigm." *SAGAR.* (Spring 2004): 105-121.

_____ "The Linear Hierarchy of the Indus 'Fish' Sign." *SAGAR.* (Spring 2005): 71-79

Koskenniemi, Kimmo and Asko Parpola. *Corpus of Texts in the Indus Script.* Helenski: Department of Asian and African Studies: University of Helenski, Research Reports No. 1, 1979.

_____. *Documentation and Duplicates in the Indus Script.* Helenski: Department of Asian and African Studies: University of Helenski, Research Reports No. 2, 1980.

_____. *A Concordance to the Texts in the Indus Script.* Helenski: Department of Asian and African Studies: University of Helenski, Research Reports No. 3, 1982.

Lal, B.B. "The Indus Script: Some Observations Based on Archaeology." *Journal of the Royal Asiatic Society of Great Britain and Ireland* (July 1973): 173-177.

Mahadevan, Iravatham. *The Indus Script: Texts, Concordance and Tables.* New Delhi: K.P. Puthran at Tata Press Limited, 1977.

_____. "Terminal Ideograms in the Indus Script." In *Harappan Civilization: A Contemporary Perspective.* ed. Gregory Possehl. New Delhi: Movian Primlani, Oxford University Press & IBH Publishing, 1982.

_____. "Aryan or Dravidian or Neither: A Study of Recent Attempts to Decipher the Indus Script." *Electronic Journal of Vedic Studies* Vol.8, Issue 1 (March 2002). Available from http://users.primushost.com/~india/ejvs/ejvs0801/ejvs0801.txt

_____. "Toward a Grammar of the Indus Texts: 'Intelligible to the Eye, not to the Ears." *Tamil Civilization* Vol. 4, nos. 3-4 (December 1986): 15-30.

_____. "Study of the Indus Script Through Bi-lingual Parallels." In *Ancient Cities of the Indus,* ed. Gregory Possehl, 261-267. New Delhi: Vikas Publishing House, 1979.

Marshall, John. *Mohenjo-Daro and the Indus Civilization.* 1931 Reprint, 3 vols. New Delhi: J. Jetley for Asian Educational Services, 1996.

Masica, Colin P. "Aryan and Non-Aryan in North Indian Agriculture." In *Aryan and Non-Aryan in India,* ed. Madhav M. Deshpande and Peter E. Hook, Michigan Papers on South and Southeast Asia No. 14, 55-151. Ann Arbor: The University of Michigan Center for South and Southeast Asian Studies, 1978.

Mitchiner, John E. *Studies in the Indus Valley Inscriptions.* New Delhi: Oxford University Press & IBH Publishing Co., 1978.

Nissen, Hans J., Peter Damerow, and Robert Englund, eds. *Archaic Bookkeeping: Early Writing and Techniques of Economic Administration in the Ancient Near East.* Translated by Paul Larsen. Chicago: University of Chicago Press, 1993.

Parpola, Asko. *Deciphering the Indus Script.* Cambridge: Cambridge University Press, 1994.

_____. "Tasks, Methods and Results in the Study of the Indus Script." *Journal of the Royal Asiatic Society of Great Britain and Ireland* (25-27 July 1973): 178-209.

_____. "Interpreting the Indus Script." In *Frontiers of the Indus Civilization,* ed. B.B. Lal and S.P. Gupta, 179-191. New Delhi: Books and Books, 1984.

Possehl, Gregory. *Indus Age: The Writing System.* Philadelphia: University of Pennsylvania Press, 1996.

_____. *Indus Age: The Beginnings.* Philadelphia: University of Pennsylvania Press, 1999.

_____. *The Indus Civilization: A Contemporary Perspective.* Walnut Creek: Altamira Press, 2002.

Potts, Daniel T. "Distant Shores: Ancient Near Eastern Trade with South Asia and Northeast Africa." In *The Civilizations of the Ancient Near East* ed. Jack M. Sasson. 3:1451-62. New York: Macmillan, 1995.

Shah, Sayid Ghulam Mustafa and Asko Parpola, eds. *Corpus of Indus Seals and Inscriptions: Collections in Pakistan.* Helsinki: Suomalainen Tiedeakatemia, 1991.

Wheeler, Sir Mortimer. *The Indus Civilization: Supplementary Volume to the Cambridge History of India.* Cambridge: Cambridge University Press, 1979.

_____. *Civilizations of the Indus Valley and Beyond.* New York: McGraw-Hill, 1966.

Wilson, J.V. Kinnier. *Indo Sumerian: A New Approach to the Problems of the Indus Script.* Oxford: Clarendon, 1974.

_____. "The Case for Accountancy." In *Frontiers of the Indus Civilization*, ed. B.B. Lal and S.P. Gupta, 173-177. New Delhi: Books and Books, 1984.

Witzel, Michael. "The Languages of Harappa: Early Linguistic Data and the Indus Civilization." In *Proceedings of the Conference on the Indus Civilization.* ed. Jonathan Mark Kenoyer, Madison: University of Wisconsin Press, 1998 (In press). Provisional copy available from www.people.fas.harvard.edu/~witzel/IndusLang.pdf.

Zide, Arlene R.K. "A Brief Survey of Work to Date on the Indus Script." In *Ancient Cities of the Indus,* ed. Gregory Possehl, 256-260. New Delhi: Vikas Publishing House, 1979.

Zide, Arlene R. K. and Kamil V. Zvelebil., eds. *The Soviet Decipherment of the Indus Valley Script: Translation and Critique.* The Hague: Mouton & Co. B. V., 1976.

APPENDIX A: THE STRUCTURAL MODEL

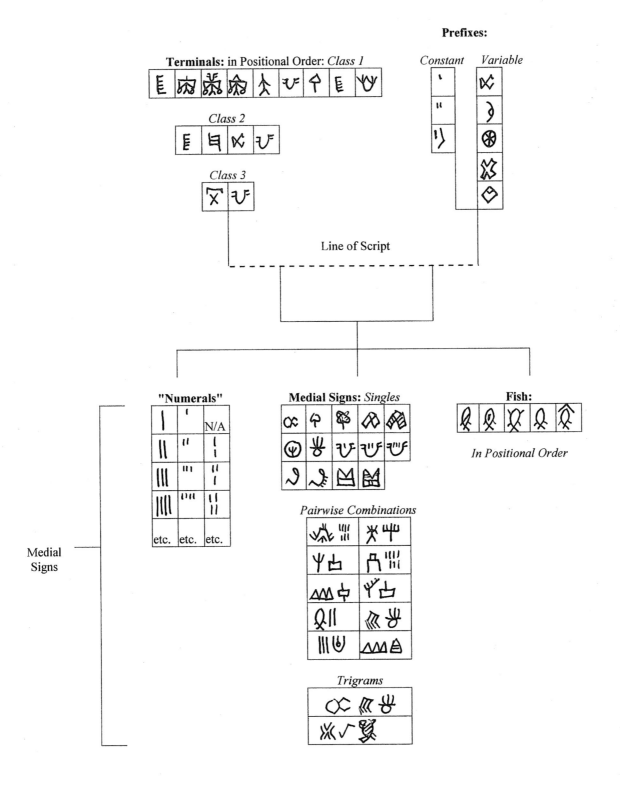

APPENDIX B: REFERENCE TO SIGNS IN THE TEXT

Prefixing Signs: Page 18

Constant Signs		Variable Signs
'		⋉
''	+	∫
''		⊗
		✕
		◇
		Other Signs Caused to be Prefixed By Constant Signs

The "Fish" Signs: Page 36				

Other Isolated Medial Signs			
Sign	Page	Sign	Page
⟨⟩	45		55
	49		41
	49		42
	56		43
	56		47
	49		52
	45		53
	35		38
	35		45
	35		57
	53		52
	53		46
	55		51

APPENDIX B (CONT.): REFERENCE TO SIGNS IN THE TEXT

Numerals: Page 59

Terminals: Page 28

Lightning Source UK Ltd.
Milton Keynes UK
UKOW03f1235191214

243416UK00002B/24/P